You ARE Your Career

REFLECT WHO YOU ARE IN THE WORK YOU DO

E. CHARLES BLISS

FIRST EDITION 2008

You ARE Your Career: Reflect who you are in the work you do

DISCLAIMER: The case studies and "real life" illustrations used throughout this book are based, in part, upon true events; but, for dramatic reasons, certain liberties have been taken with names, **places, dates and circumstances.** Therefore, any actions, motivations, **or opinions attributed to actual people are** fictional and are presented solely for educational purposes.

First Edition, First Printing
Printed in United States of America

Email: blissed2@gmail.com

DEDICATION

This book is dedicated to SUED.

To: Melissa

Enjoy as you will —

Edwin

ACKNOWLEDGMENTS

I would like to acknowledge Wendy Freeman who gave me a chance to do this work, mentored me in the profession of career counseling and who provides ongoing support and encouragement. My fellow workers Christine Wagner, Mychael Heuer, Kathy Anderson and Barbara Determan have been valuable members of the Career Development team where new ideas and approaches are born every day.

My thanks to my numerous editors and contributors and those who let me tell their stories: John Ford, Niki Amarantides, Scott Allen Stevens, Lena Kline-Shedd, Stacia Lewis, Pat Thon, Terrie Bjork, Ralph Mackey, the late Duane Watkins (gone but certainly not forgotten.), Cynthia Harris, Stephanie Brooks.

My wife Susan has been a rock throughout the process of writing this book. She has functioned as an editor, a contributor, a sounding board, a supporter, a critic and my partner.

CONTENTS

PREFACE

In my work as a career counselor I meet many people who can't seem to get their career started or are unhappy with their career choices. I wrote this book to consolidate many of the things I've learned about how to help people find a better fit between who they are as a person and the work they pursue. It is based on the premise that what you value in your life is key to projecting yourself into satisfying work—paid employment, self-employment, small business employment and/or volunteer employment. As you find out more about yourself, finding a compatible career becomes much easier.

There are many books on the market that promise an easy, trouble free way to accomplish all of your life goals. The problem is that many people have no clear idea about what their life goals are, much less a strategy to actualize them. This book is an attempt to help you find clarity about what you *want* to do and create a plan to get it done.

Introduction

LIFE = CAREER. It *really* is as simple as that! Most people have a narrow view of what it means to have a career—they think career equals their job, but I encourage you to expand your understanding of the word career. There are at least three definitions of career: a job, a life path, or a journey. The long version of my new definition is: *Career is the sum total of everything you do in your life*. Career is not just your job, but includes it. Career includes your volunteer activities and your family relationships—every aspect of your life is included. This is a radical way to look at the concept of career to be sure, but in the course of reading this book you will see that it frees you up to consider all facets of your life when thinking about your career. If your life is in order, your career will be in order.

I approach the writing of this book not so much from a technical angle, but from a human one, although I will give you plenty of exercises and references to use. However, *only you can decide what you want to do with your life*. I will introduce you to a system of thinking about your life and career. This system helps you find the threads that connect all aspects of your life. You will do this by examining some life systems: values, ambitions, resources, balance, and relationships. Although you will work with each of these systems separately to gain clarity, a more dynamic YOU can only be created by connecting the systems. A lofty goal, but achievable,

The exercises are interesting, fun (I hope) and will assist you in discovering *your* answers as you gain knowledge about yourself. Each chapter of the book is designed to move you progressively from dreams about your desired future, to the accumulation of resources needed to move forward with the dream, and finally to an action plan to implement your dream. It's a developmental process that threads together the most important elements of your dream into a beautiful life/career quilt.

Your dream is like a computer you buy and bring home from the store. As long as the computer is in the box, it is just a dream. It represents unrealized potential. When it is hooked up (activated), it becomes a reality. To assert your will in life, to be persistent enough to cause something important to happen in your life, to take action in your own behalf is like hooking up the computer.

The decisions you make on a day-to-day basis will determine whether or not you have a successful life/career. A successful life/career can only be defined by you. But once you can figure out what you want, you can have it. This book will show you how, by introducing you to the Dream It, Learn It, Work It system. Many writers of self-help books suggest you have to do it their way or no way. I believe you already know more about yourself than you are aware of consciously and you just have to find a way to tap into that knowledge. Whatever method works for you is the right one.

You will figure out your own personal definition of success as well as create a picture of what your success will look like, how it will feel. You will learn how to set *achievable* goals along the way (a straight-forward process in my system) and how to adjust your goals as your idea of success shifts from time to time—and it will, believe me. You will learn about creating the resources you will need and how to maintain a balanced life, and you will see how each thread of your life affects every other thread. The philosopher Aristotle wrote about the Golden Mean, an ideal between two extremes. The path you find for yourself that is just the right path for you— the golden middle path leading to your picture of success. You will find the Golden Mean in your own life.

Once you have completed the "what" for your life, we will deal with the "how." I must repeat here that knowing what you want is the most difficult challenge. Armed with that knowledge, how to achieve it is often a step-by-step process. Author Claude Bristol in his book, "The Magic of Believing," suggests whatever you can believe, you can achieve. Other writers, before and since, have said similar things, but Bristol says it as clearly as it can be said.

So here we are at the starting point of a great adventure—the rest of your life. As a career professional, I have engaged in this exploration with many people. You will read stories of real people who have used the tools in this book. You will see that many paths lead to life/career success, but that only you can find the right path to your own dream. No two people are alike, or even close to being alike. No two careers are the same; no two lives are lived the same way. But there *is* a way, a way that is *the* right way for you. Welcome!

CHAPTER 1:

Know Thyself

"Know thyself"—Socrates' directive provides the short answer to the complex question of personal assessment. If you are looking to find an occupation that matches the purposes of your life, you must begin by looking at yourself from the inside out. Looking at all the possibilities that exist in the world and then figuring out the one that will work for you is nearly impossible. I wouldn't say it never happens, because I have known people who knew even at an early age what they wanted to do occupationally. I don't know how that happened, but I do know it is rare. For most of us, figuring out who we are keeps us busy throughout much of our life. So if you figure out who you are and what you value, you will be a long way toward knowing what occupation (or just what plain old job for that matter) will likely work for you.

Most people, however, do not have such innate clarity about their career. In places where jobs requiring little formal education are available, young men and women often go to work for the dominant industry in the area. I went to school in eastern Washington State, where a significant number of my classmates went to Seattle after graduation to work for The Boeing Company. Boeing always seemed to have openings in a wide selection of job categories, the pay was good, opportunities for advancement were abundant, and moving from a small town to the big city of Seattle was an adventure. The availability of jobs in a geographic area often obviates the need for people to really think about and figure

1

out what might be the best job fit for them. They are looking for a job, they find a job, they make decent wages—life is good. In the past, this course of action was all that was needed to secure near-permanent or permanent employment until retirement. Today the world of work is much more precarious. The chances of working for only one employer from start to retirement are increasingly rare. A few years ago, employees joked about working for a single employer from "womb to tomb." Government may be one of the few places where lifetime employment might still happen—but that's dwindling, too.

Some people graduate from high school or college and take the first job to come their way. Often it is not the occupation of their choosing, but it is convenient and feels like a good place to start. Once again, this is not a carefully planned decision about employment, but a decision of availability and necessity—when you get out of school you go get a job, right? First jobs can stretch into long-term jobs quite easily for many reasons. You are receiving a steady paycheck, you now have regular living expenses to meet, you like your boss, there are some limited opportunities for promotion, and you are successfully doing the job. It seems the longer you stay, the more difficult it is to think about leaving. Seeking new employment while currently working is challenging. You may not have even thought about what you really want to do with your life/career because you feel you're doing just fine.

The two scenarios I just described fall into the category of accidental jobs. Somehow they just happened. In either situation, life may seem good until the day comes when either the company lays you off, usually with little notice, or you wake up one morning hating your job, hating your life, and realizing you have stayed too long. This is the moment, a moment of truth if you will, when people begin to think about their lives in broader terms and begin to speculate about the meaning of their lives. Questioning your life work can happen at mid-life, but not necessarily. It usually happens when you have taken on the normal responsibilities and financial commitments of adult life. Unemployment rarely happens at the right time. More often it happens at exactly the worst time. Pressure builds all around you. You may be virtually paralyzed with fear; fear that you will never find another job, fear that you have no marketable skills, fear that will you lose everything you own, fear that others will judge you a loser, and fear that all hope is gone and you are helpless to do anything about it. Have you ever found yourself in this situation? Most of us have. Believe it or not, this is a perfect time for change and renewal. In a time of crisis, you've effectively been "painted into a corner;" forcing you to "paint your way out" by adapting.

Think for just a moment about a time you had to make a change you really did not want make. Reflect on what you did to cope. Fear can cripple you only if you have no idea about what to do next. You don't have to figure out the rest of your life, just one step you can take immediately to begin moving in a new direction. So in thinking about employment, if you have a sense of what you are looking for and what likely will work for you, then you can at least ask appropriate questions about your next job.

Even when you start out in the perfect new work environment, changes in co-workers or in management can cause a dramatic shift in working conditions. It can happen overnight. Knowing *who you are* will help you recognize these situations when they occur and in most cases you can adjust. In other cases, you may be so incompatible with these new circumstances that making a move to a better situation is the best solution. Sadly, most people don't make such moves. They learn to compromise; they "bite the bullet," learn to live with the new circumstances, and hope they can outlast the work conditions that are driving them nuts. Which way do *you* usually adjust? Are you a person who would be better off compromising and waiting it out? Or are you someone who would be better off moving on? Self-knowledge will point you to the right path.

One possibility may be to find a new job within the same organization with more compatible co-workers and/or bosses. Many of us become economically trapped in our jobs; we are so dependent on our paycheck that we cannot imagine voluntarily leaving our job and possibly reducing our income. This is a tough problem to deal with, but there are financial strategies that can ease your burden, allowing you more freedom of movement in your search. If you are not economically trapped, you obviously have more options.

How do you find out what you need to know about yourself in order to make good life/career decisions? Current research tells us that a person may have at least four to seven occupations in a lifetime, some of them unrelated to others. If so, what is the common denominator in all those occupations? The answer: YOU. Knowing who you are and how you make your life meaningful is absolutely critical in the process of finding what Buddhists call "right livelihood."

Making meaning in your life means making sense out of what you are doing *in the larger context of your life*. What are your beliefs, values, attitudes, concerns, wants, needs, talents and skills? What must be in your life for you to experience *satisfaction* each day? How do you find these things out?

Fortunately, myriad tools exist to help you reflect on and complete a personal assessment of your life. Some people use the processes of counseling and psychotherapy to discover meaning in their lives. Many engage in these processes not because they have a particular problem, but because they seek a deeper understanding of self. Some use their religion or spirituality as the bedrock of their belief system and seek guidance through the teachings or clergy of their faith. Some people write in diaries and keep journals to capture elusive insights about themselves. For others, just talking with a good friend helps find clarity. Most of us seek a unique path that works for us. And these methods often work well, at least for a period of time. *But how do you make life/career decisions that will sustain you?*

To get you started on personal assessment and to prove to you there are many things you would like to do in your life, things that you have thought about but have not done, I would like for you to think about three things you *want* to do in your life or career and write them down.

EXERCISE: THREE THINGS I WANT TO DO

#1: _____

#2: _____

#3: _____

You may find this an easy exercise that allows you to put in writing something you have thought about for a long time, but never acted on. Or you may draw a big blank and be unable to think of one single idea to list, let alone three. If you had no trouble writing down three ideas, you are probably ready to move on to Chapter 2 and begin to refine them. If you found it difficult, or impossible to complete the writing, or if you just want more insight, try the Life Values Rating exercise which follows.

EXERCISE: LIFE VALUES RATING

In this Life Values Rating exercise, you will weigh nine different options in considering your life values. I will identify and name them, explain what each one means, and then have you rate your interest in them.

Below each description is a scale from 1 to 10. Rate your level of interest in each of the nine life values. When you are done, each value will have been rated from 1 to 10. This is a time to be honest with yourself. Do not rate values high because you think you should. Don't rate them low just because you can't see how you could possibly attain them. The point of this book is to help you look at what you really *want* in your life and to develop strategies to get you there. We do it step-by-step and mile-by-mile. This is an early, but extremely important step. Please complete the exercise now by circling a number from 1 (low interest) to 10 (high interest) that reflects your true interest in each life value.

Life Value #1—Work/Job/Occupation: the work/job value is the value you want if you are a work-oriented person or you are at a time in your life when your occupation is most important to you. Work/job includes both being employed by others and/or being employed by yourself, either through self-employment or business ownership.

1   2   3   4   5   6   7   8   9   10

Life Value #2—Financial/Material Well-Being: the financial/material value is important if achieving wealth in your life and having extensive material possessions are of prime concern. This value passes beyond safety and comfort in your life and leads to riches and glory in your life and your surroundings.

1   2   3   4   5   6   7   8   9   10

Life Value #3—Self-Development/Education: You may be most interested in the value that leads to self-knowledge and intellectual challenge. This may be a value you pursue at various times in your life or it may always be one of your primary values.

1   2   3   4   5   6   7   8   9   10

Life Value #4—Creativity: creativity encourages you to use your artistic and creative talents to complete meaningful art (visual art, performing art, writing) projects or to apply your creative skills to solve difficult problems. The emphasis is on the creative process.

1   2   3   4   5   6   7   8   9   10

Life Value #5—Family/Relationships/Love: Perhaps nurturing and maintaining strong family ties is the interest you are destined to follow. Family/relationships include friendships and social relationships. If you choose this route you are undoubtedly a lover of people and will rarely travel alone.

1   2   3   4   5   6   7   8   9   10

Life Value #6—Health/Beauty/Fitness: This leads to a place that values personal health above all. To get to personal health you must travel through the fitness camp. Beauty has almost always gone along with health and fitness. This trail may be especially attractive as you begin the transition from youth to adult maturity.

1   2   3   4   5   6   7   8   9   10

Life Value #7—Recreation/Adventure/Travel: Recreation/travel will certainly be a secondary value for many people, but a few people want it to be the primary focus in their lives. This value can lead to a career or a life of seeking adventure and experiencing new places.

1   2   3   4   5   6   7   8   9   10

Life Value #8—Spiritual: Spiritual is the path to your belief system. Whatever you believe to be true will guide your actions and decisions. Some people want to follow the spiritual life and will sacrifice greatly to do so.

1   2   3   4   5   6   7   8   9   10

Life Value #9—Service: The life value of service zigzags across all the other values because seekers of this value want to help. They want to be of service to others because they are themselves rewarded when people they help are successful.

1   2   3   4   5   6   7   8   9   10

After you have completed the Life Values Rating exercise, compile your results in the summary chart below. Write down the names of the life values you rated in each of the 10 rating options. How many values did you rate at 10? Write the life value name or names beside the appropriate rating number. How many values did you rate at 9? Write in the life value name or names. There will likely be some rating numbers you do not use and some you use more than once. That's fine.

Compiling Results of the Life Value Rating Exercise

Rating Number   Life Value Name(s)

Rating Number	Life Value Name(s)
10	_____
9	_____
8	_____
7	_____
6	_____
5	_____
4	_____
3	_____
2	_____
1	_____

Good! Each life value should have a rating number next to it. To complete this exercise, the results of which we will be using as we move forward, please identify the three life values that have the highest ratings. For example, if Life Value #1 (Work/Career/Occupation) is rated 10, and your next highest rating is 8 for Life Value #6 (Health/Beauty/Fitness) and Life Value #7 (Recreation/Travel/Adventure), then those are your top three life values at this time. If you have more that one life value rated at 10, you must decide which life value is most important to you right now so we can complete the last part of the exercise.

Next you see a diagram showing your primary life value, and the two other alternate life values of great importance to you. Complete the exercise by completing this final diagram.

The example I just used will look like this:

Primary Life Value   #1:   Work/Career/Occupation

Second Life Value   #7:   Recreation/Travel/Adventure

Third Life Value   #6:   Health/Beauty/Fitness

Now complete your own diagram.

My Primary Life Value is #		
My Second Life Value #		
My Third Life Value is #		

Excellent. You have just completed the Life Values Rating exercise and gained some insight about yourself. We will be using the results of this exercise later in the book so if you have not yet done it, please take a few minutes, go back and complete the Life Values Rating exercise now.

So to summarize where we are and where we are going, I assume you are reading this book because you want to change something in your life. You are either uncomfortable, dissatisfied or you want to improve some aspect of your life. I am asking you to listen to and heed your uneasiness and/or desires, identify elements of your life you want to work on (having found them in the Life Values Rating exercise) and together we will organize a process to help you move in a new direction.

If you're interested in exploring other assessment exercises and tools, see Appendix 1: Additional Resources for Assessment.

Final Thoughts

Has this exercise helped you to reconnect with something that has been missing in your life? Perhaps you feel a certain void that needs to be filled or remember a dream you have not accomplished. *Do you have an itch you can't scratch? What is the thing you have always done in your life that you are not doing now?* These are potential clues to discovering your life's purpose, over and above the mundane concerns of daily living. Sometimes we get so caught up in living our lives that we neglect to take time to reflect on the meaning of our lives. Why *are* you here on planet earth and what higher purpose can you serve? Only you can determine the answer to these questions, but this book can serve as a toolkit that will not only help you discover your calling, but assist you to move your life in a direction that has great promise and hope.

Beware of "Shoulding"

For some reason many people who are naturally drawn in a certain direction in their lives—art or music, for example—are discouraged from following this inner call because it "comes too easy." Many believe that if something is difficult for us to do, it is somehow more valuable. I say NONSENSE. Albert Ellis, renowned psychologist, whose work I recommend to you, says the struggle in life is often between your "shoulds" and your "wants." He warns people that "shoulding" all over the place (and yourself) may leave you miserable. So if you are a musician, but you are working as an accountant because you think you should, you may want to think about *why*. Don't categorically eliminate what you are inclined to do or what you find easy or enjoyable in favor of something more difficult. And don't assume that the difficult thing you are reaching for is a guarantee of success or virtue. Even if you are discouraged from pursuing what you are naturally drawn to, it is amazing how often you find a way to incorporate it into your life, whether you recognize it or not.

CHAPTER 2:

Dream It: Reflection as Preparation for Action

The work suggested so far is difficult to do because it asks you to reflect on and prioritize what is most important in your life at this moment. It means you have to make choices that you may not want to make. A commitment to knowing yourself and consciously deciding the direction of your career and your life can be a huge challenge. *Don't procrastinate or think that you're not ready. Remember that your decisions will never be perfect—never exactly right—but they must be made so you can move forward.*

You may find yourself in a position where you must make the best decision you can for yourself without having all the information you want. Furthermore, you may make a choice that does not work or one that you may change in the future. Use your best information and make a conscious choice so you can move on with the process of life/career discovery. If you can't make a choice, then take a guess at what your choice might be if you were able to make it and go with that as a temporary choice. With luck, you will be convinced during the course of reading this book that knowing your life's direction and making conscious decisions about yourself is the starting point for all good things.

Years ago, I was stunned when I read "Choice Theory," a book written by psychiatrist William Glasser. I understood the essence of his theory to be that we always have choices in life and we can make conscious choices about how we want to live our lives. It seemed too simple. I questioned whether I believed this to be true. I finally realized I needed to think about his ideas within the context of change. If I wanted to make a change in my life, *that* was the decision I had to make first, *even before deciding exactly what that change might be.* Nobody can make you change if you don't want to and that is why you are the writer, director, producer and star actor in your own life/career movie. Only you can tie it all together and I encourage you to realize your power and script it *large.*

In addition to the Life Values Ratings exercise, many techniques may help you discover the sometimes-illusive notion of what you were put on this earth to do—to contemplate your life work. I believe you already know what you would like to do; the thing that expresses who you are, but you may not have found a means of transition *yet.* If this is the case for you, then you have crossed one big hurdle and will be ready for the exercises later in this chapter. If you do not know yet what you would like to do with your life/career, to discover your calling, let me suggest a few more good ways to try to find out. I can't say with any degree of certainty which method or idea will work best for you—we are all so different. But I do know that the methods I am suggesting have helped many people gain some insight about what they want to do next in their lives.

Contemplation

A powerful and profound exercise is to simply sit in a quiet place and think about who you are (the part that you know). Become as relaxed as you can, and just dream a little about who you are and what it means. Do not seek instant answers. Just open yourself to listening and hearing yourself and see what happens.

In North American culture, we are generally taught that if we want something, we just quickly go out and get it, by any means necessary. We learn to quest for things in an aggressive way. We feel a need to be successful in the way society defines success and we often feel great pressure to perform—compete in sports, succeed at work, acquire bigger and better "things," get good grades, consume more of the good life, run for office, become a professional, or learn a trade. The implication is that you must reach out, grab, and then hold onto the things you want.

However, this model does not work for everyone and is not always a good way to get in touch with yourself and your true needs and desires. The process I am talking about is one of letting go, not grasping and hanging on for dear life. It is counterintuitive for most of us to just let go, or to let go and listen. We are very good at actively pursuing and making noise. I encourage you to let go of expectations (your own and others') and listen. I have done this a few times in my life, primarily by being quiet and meditating. I am amazed at how relaxed and open I can become when I am able to "hear myself" in this practice. How about you? Do you have a formal way of getting in touch with yourself, do you have a favorite place you go for contemplation, do you know how to look inside when you want to, can you get in touch with you? *This might be a really good time to close this book and give it a try.*

If you need help relaxing and listening, you might try a system called "progressive relaxation" that is practiced in psychology and behavioral health. With or without the aid of a biofeedback mechanism, you are encouraged to learn to relax your body. The belief of this theory is that the body and the mind are not separate, but function as a whole. Therefore, say the practitioners, if you learn to relax your body you will automatically learn to relax your mind. If your mind is relaxed, you may be able to get in touch with your deeper self. You probably will need some help from a biofeedback practitioner to get started, but the results may be well worth the time, effort and expense. When I used biofeedback a few years ago, I was startled to learn that I really could not tell when my muscles were tense and when they were relaxed until I was trained in this method.

Other approaches that might encourage relaxation and letting go include Yoga, Tai Chi, meditation, deep breathing, exercise, and visualization. I will not discuss these in detail because you can find out all about them by doing a little creative research. Later in the book, we'll talk more about creative resource development.

Dreaming

Remember, as you did in the previous chapter, who you are at a deep level and imagine what you might do with your life to add meaning. Now can you imagine yourself doing the new thing? As you were reflecting on your life, being in touch with your desires, letting go and listening to your inner self, what exciting dream presented itself? Can you visualize yourself being the principle actor in your own dream? Visualizing your idea or dream as though it were already realized adds powerful subconscious motivation to take the next step.

You might want to write about it in your journal or notebook, maybe you'll want to draw a picture of yourself doing "your new thing." Perhaps you'll want to meditate about it, visualize yourself doing it, or write yourself a letter dated five years in the future where you explain to yourself how you got to where you are and especially how you felt about the journey.

Just hold this picture or thought in your mind, do it often, sleep on it at night, dream about it during the day and do it with a positive attitude. I would caution you to be careful about whom you share your idea with, because many people (even loved ones) may not understand what you are trying to do or may try to pour cold water on your idea. Since you are just at the beginning of this process, the one thing you do not need are negative messages. As you progress, you will, of course, need to share more with the important people in your life. As with anything that is newly born, your dream must be nurtured and protected until it achieves some maturity. Everyone will probably handle this a little bit differently, but remember critics come in large numbers from all directions, while those who would encourage and support you in a positive manner are often few and they must be treasured.

So now, let's expand on the idea you are trying to pursue. Describe your specific idea in as much detail as possible. For example, if you want to open a small business in your own home, then you must know *exactly* what kind of business it will be. You need to be able to *see* it.

EXERCISE: MY DREAM (I)

My dream for my life/career looks like this:

_____

_____

_____

_____

_____

_____

_____

_____

_____

_____

_____

If you found that space frighteningly blank and skipped over it, you may need to work a little more on defining your dream/idea. The next exercise will help you do that, helping you find clarity even if you already have a goal in mind.

EXERCISE: 10 THINGS

Write down ten things you always wanted to do. These can be jobs you want to do, occupations you want to investigate or, even better, any ten things you want to do in your life. It can be anything from getting married and raising children to climbing a mountain.

Ten Things I've Always Wanted to Do

1. _____

2. _____

3. _____

4. _____

5. _____

6. _____

7. _____

8. _____

9. _____

10. _____

Now look over your list and cross out the three things that are least important to you. It isn't that they are unimportant, but at this time they are not as important as the seven remaining items. Now, of the seven remaining items, choose the three that you want to do the most. And there you go—from ten to three, just like that. You probably realize that this is just another way to get at or validate the "Three Things I Want to Do" exercise in Chapter 1. Of the three items that made your final list, put them in the order of their importance, understanding that the number one item is the one you are going to do first, as in immediately.

Employment Types

Once you have come to know more about life/career direction, it's time to examine what you can do to make a meaningful occupational choice. The definition of occupation I am using in this book includes four types of jobs:

1. Self-Employed

3. Small Business Owner

3. Employee in a Small, Medium or Large Organization

4. Volunteer

You may want to create a hybrid of these three job types by combining them in interesting ways. You do not have to choose one to the exclusion of all others—but a primary choice is probably necessary in order to focus your energy, at least in the beginning.

On Self Employment

The reason I mention small business owners (or self-employment) is because almost everyone I have ever met has some notion of what they would do if they were in business for themselves.

I once managed a program encouraging low-income people to explore the possibility of turning one of their ideas into a business. It was amazing to see how many people knew what they wanted to do and in some cases had done on a very small scale. With a little bit of coaching, some business education, and a lot of encouragement, many of the program participants were able to start a business or expand a hobby into a business opportunity. I do not mention this because I want everyone to become self-employed, but to illustrate that we all have ideas about how we can be successful, whether we are rich or poor.

Another way to look at our lives is to say that all of us are self-employed in the sense that we must manage all aspects of our lives (our career) in order to return a profit; no family or business can survive long without a return on investment. If you happen to be employed by a company that pays you wages, then wages are one source of income for your family (business), but certainly not the only source. So just as an idea, you might want to think about running your life as a business and make sure you are running a profitable enterprise. Not all profits will be in the form of money; some of the best profits come from the intangibles that make your life important.

Exercise: Occupational Direction, or "Where Do I Fit In?"

Here is a quick way to get some direction about your occupational choices. Read through the occupational categories listed below and check-off the one(s) that fit (or *feel* like they fit) your dream.

1. ____Management, business and/or financial operations
2. ____Professional occupations (includes creative work)
3. ____Sales
4. ____Office and administrative support
5. ____Service (includes police and fire fighters)
6. ____Farming, fishing and forestry
7. ____Installation, maintenance and repair
8. ____Construction trades
9. ____Production, assembly and fabrication
10. ____Transportation

Favorite occupational area:_____

Favorite way to be employed:

1. Self-employed
2. Small business owner
3. Employee working for others in a small, medium or large organization
4. Volunteer

You say you want to explore occupational areas in more depth? I'm happy to oblige. See the Occupational Direction Exercise in Appendix 2.

Chapters 1 and 2 have been all about deciding which dream you want to pursue, the idea you want to develop, the job you want to do. Either because you already knew what you wanted to do and were seeking confirmation or because you figured it out using some of the exercises and suggestions, you should now have a pretty good idea about what you want to do. So let's move on and really begin to lock your desired future into your "conscious thoughts."

CHAPTER 3:

Learn It: Getting from *What to Why?*

Your project is now started. At the least you have thought about what you want to do and at the best you have decided exactly *what* you want to do. Hallelujah! Now listen up. If you are reading this book straight through without actually doing things I am suggesting as we move along, that's fine. But when you get serious about doing whatever it is you decide you want to do, then you must resolve for yourself *why* you are going to be doing what you are going to do. After all, this process has the potential to change your life in significant and sometimes *irreversible* ways and you better know *why you're doing it*. Let's begin with a plausible scenario.

Susan, a stay-at-home mother, wants to make specialty soaps to sell locally because she loves doing "crafty things" and because she would like to contribute to the family income. This idea works for her because she sees herself as a helpmate to her husband and a stay-at-home mom to her children. But she also knows she loves to be creative and make things that are useful. She has decided making soap is a great idea because she believes she can do it at home and because the initial investment of money will probably be very small. What does she need to get started?

Susan obviously needs the support of her family, so she needs to talk it over with both her husband and her children. Assuming she gets their concurrence and hopefully, loving support, she must now find: how to make soap, room to make it, how to package the soap, how to manage a small home business, and how to market her product. All of these elements must be in place if she is to succeed in the long run with the soap-making business. Where should she start?

There are several places she could go to learn about making soap. The local library, searching the Internet, local classes at a church or craft store, talking to stores that sell specialty soap, buying some specialty soap and conducting a chemical analysis of it, and talking to her grandmother who made soap for years are all possibilities. One thing is sure; if she is going to sell soap, she will have to learn how to make soap. This may take a little while or a long while. It is the logical place to start and she must do this first.

Assuming she will receive the support of her family, she can also begin to look at other issues while she is learning to make soap. She can begin to create a soap-making space in her home. She can peruse novelty and gift shops that sell soap and get an idea of packaging and pricing. She can take a class at the community college and learn how to manage a small business in her community. Finally, although this may be covered in her business class, she can research various methods of selling her soap once she learns to make it. The first priority is learning to make the soap, but she can also pursue other learning at the same time, or if she wants to, she can just do these things in sequential order and arrive at the same place, just a little later.

Why = The Commitment that Sustains You

For all but a few of us, knowing what we want to do is not very risky if we keep the idea to ourselves, daydream about it from time to time, share it as a fantasy with a few friends, and never tell ourselves why we might actually want to do it. Accepting some risk is the price of admission into the processes I am describing. If *what* is the engine driving our process, then *why* is the fuel that keeps it going.

So how do you keep it going, how do you maintain momentum when there are many forces in your life that might impede you? How do you keep going when a family emergency happens, when there are increasing demands on your time, when money for your project could be used elsewhere? The answer is commitment. Commitment comes if the reasons (the why) that fuel your plan are very solid and you believe in them. If you are truly committed to your plan, you will find a way. No matter how distracted you may become, you will find a way to come back to the project. Remember that this is your dream, this is your career, and this is your life. This becomes a vital part of who you are.

It is not sufficient to say you are committed and to think you know why you are changing your life. You must have an almost overwhelming feeling of satisfaction thinking about what you are about to do. It helps to be able to articulate clearly what you are doing and why. I am deliberately repeating myself to emphasize the importance of this point. Are you ready for the "what and why" test? Here it is.

EXERCISE: THE WHAT AND WHY TEST:

Write three sentences that clearly explain exactly *what* you plan to do and *why* you plan to change your life/career. Use action words to give life to your thoughts. You might use this format: I want to do (what) for the following reasons (why).

Sentence #1: _____

_____

_____ .

Sentence #2: _____

_____

_____ .

Sentence #3:_____

_____

_____ .

Let's go back to Susan the soap-making mother to see how this might work out. Let's assume that she found out how to make soap, found a place to make soap, and even began to make soap. But she is unhappy with the soap she is making because it is not pretty enough and the scents are just not right. She begins to think nobody will want to buy her soap because it is not good enough, and no one will be willing to pay her a price that would cover her inventory cost to make the soap, let alone pay her a reasonable amount of money for her time. She may be right. This is often how these adventures begin and why so many people become discouraged and give up. However, if you are armed with the knowledge that "ain't nothing easy," then you will expect the bumps in the road that you are bound to encounter. This is the reason that knowing exactly *what* you are attempting and *why* you are attempting it are so important.

Here is how Susan might write her three sentences:

Sentence #1: I want to make a useful product (soap) that I can sell to make money for my family and I prefer remaining at home and being available to my children and my husband.

Sentence #2: I want to engage myself in a creative process that requires me to learn many new skills, such as business management, soap making, and marketing because I love a challenge, I will be setting a good example for my children and I will control all facets of the process.

Sentence #3: I want to explore a part of my being that has been dormant for several years and thrill to the delight of new discoveries about myself and soap making is the perfect vehicle to do so. Because I want to grow as my family grows, I will be able to transition my business from a start-up to a more mature business on my own terms and schedule.

Susan may have to give away a lot of soap to a lot of people before she gets her formula just right. She may also have to sell her soap below her costs (especially her own wages) until she develops a market. She may have to learn much more about soap making before she can make any money at it. She may have to invent new ways to make soap (in other words, invent her own soap making secrets) before the soap meets her own expectations. Eventually, she will develop a product, a soap, that she believes is so appealing that anyone would want to have it. She must continue to revive and sustain her dream in her mind. She must remind herself why she got started on this project in the first place. She must keep her vision clearly focused on the gem that is her dream—soap, beautiful soap, and of course endless waves of people who want to buy it. If fact, her slogan might go something like this: If I can get your hands on my soap, then my success is in your hands.

Most big businesses start very small. Just one person with an idea, perhaps a little different from anyone else's idea, but an idea that the person believes is a winner. Most of all they have the willingness to work toward making that idea a reality. It is hard to know you are going to climb Mt. Rainier, if right now you are having trouble getting up the hill behind your house. It is important, however, to keep your eye on Mt. Rainier because this larger goal will provide you with sufficient motivation to do all the things you have to do to get there.

If you continue to pursue your dream, big or small, if you can continue to find adequate resources, you will eventually meet with success. As you enjoy success, you will face other challenges. If you are pursuing self-employment or a small business you might ask, Now that I know I can make this work, is the return worth the effort? Should the business be expanded? Can I continue to do all the work myself? Do I need to add new products? Is my business taking more of my time than I want to give to it?

If you're volunteering your time in the community at large, you must determine if you are really making a difference. Does the organization(s) you plan to volunteer for have a mission you can fully support? Does volunteering add to the richness of your life?

If you are pursuing employment where you work for others, you ask yourself: Is the work as satisfying and rewarding as I hoped it would be? Am I moving up in the organization? Am I working at the correct level for my occupational aspirations? Is it time to move on?

The point is to try to make these decisions consciously instead of haphazardly. You must be thinking ahead of yourself at all times. You cannot become so wrapped up in the work that you leave no time to reflect on *what* the work should be.

Let's say that your dream is not about starting a business, but about landing a better job, maybe even your dream job. You will need to follow the same process of preparing yourself by knowing yourself, creating a dream of the job you want, doing the research, and obtaining the correct combination of education and experience to be qualified for the job. Your decision about moving forward is just the same as what you have been reading about for a business or project development. You must summon up the courage to leap from where you are to where you want to be. Although most of us might prefer to bridge from one job to another in a smooth transition (and little risk), there will always be a time when you must let go of the old and embrace the new. A smaller leap, perhaps, but a leap nonetheless. You will probably have to leave a job that is providing for you and your family reasonably well. You will have to move from the known job (even if it is not that exciting) to the unknown job with the inherent risks involved.

Some people cope with this dilemma by moving around (and usually up) within the same organization. It isn't really their dream job, but it pays better money and the change is positive, at least until the new job is mastered. Other people try to move strategically from one company or organization to the next using these moves as stepping-stones to their ideal job. All of these methods might work. Which one is most likely to work for you?

- How many times have you become complacent and rationalized that things are probably not as bad as you make them out to be?

- Are you trapped economically with no choice but to stay put or face financial ruin?

- Is being stuck in a bad job a metaphor for the rest of your life?

- Where will you find the energy to make a significant change in your employment?

- Do you see your job as a vital part of your life/career continuum?

This isn't getting any easier is it? But it is what we all face when we attempt to change our lives and take responsibility for what happens to us. Assuming responsibility for everything that has happened to you in your life as well as your reaction to all of it is very difficult, if not painful. It doesn't seem the least bit fair, especially when outside forces overwhelm your ability to control things. Many of us feel that if something is out of our control, then we cannot be held accountable. Not true. Regardless of whether or not you can control something that happens in your life, you are still responsible for your reaction and response.

I say this to point out that there are times in your life when you will be all alone, with no one else who can help you. It is at those times you must muster up the courage to do what needs to be done, or what you want to do. There are some paths in life that only you can walk, alone, and moving from dreaming about what you want to acting on those dreams, regardless of the reason you want to make a move, is one of those paths. I want to encourage you to look at the numerous examples all around you of people who have taken the harder, unknown path and how much you admire and respect them. Who stands out in your mind as someone who has overcome major obstacles in their life and moved in the direction of their dream? Are they historical figures or are they people you live and work with every day? Inspiration to act may be embodied in someone just around the next corner, or sitting in the next cubicle, or eating dinner with you, or playing ball down the road, or writing a letter from far away, or fighting a war somewhere, or preaching from a pulpit, or loving you for who you are, or even living within you as a memory. Who can provide you the inspiration to take the next step forward in your life/career?

If that person is accessible, try talking to them about your plans. If they are not accessible, for whatever reason, reflect on how they might react if they were going to do what you plan to do. Use them as a touchstone of inspiration and courage.

As you have learned in this chapter, once you start taking action, you are just beginning a long and intriguing journey. Why not make the leap of faith? Think carefully about what you have to lose by getting started. Whether you change to follow your dream or decide to stay where you are and survive, it is a long journey. Are you ready to take the next step?

Persistence to continue can be facilitated if you picture yourself successfully accomplishing your dream. See it in color and put it into motion. If you are not a visual person, try hearing or feeling your dream accomplishments. See, feel, or hear yourself not only starting to accomplish your dream, but sticking with it, running it out for the long haul. It is so much fun to put your energy into starting something you really love to do. Now that you know exactly (or almost) what you want to do, you must think about how you are going to do it and sustain it. You are mentally prepared and eager to move on, but you need some more techniques that will be discussed in the next few chapters. But before you move on, here is another exercise to help you get your dream picture just the way you want it. It is designed to consolidate/coalesce all the work you have done so far.

EXERCISE: PICTURING MY SUCCESS

My dream is _____

_____

_____ .

I keep my dream vivid and alive by_____

_____

_____ .

In my mind, I have already accomplished my dream and I am remembering how difficult it was to do and how joyful I felt as I became successful; these are some of the lessons I learned along the way

_____

_____

_____ .

I know for sure I can complete what I start; I am intelligent enough to figure out how to do it in my own way, and I will imagine my success frequently by_____

_____

_____

_____.

A great technique for adding to your visual imagery as you reflect on your success is to literally draw a picture of you being successful. Draw a picture of your personal success below.

My picture of my success in accomplishing my dream:

Closing the Circle

What you want to do and why you want to do it should be getting pretty clear by now. However, sometimes the picture cannot be fully developed until you act on a hunch, or flesh out a vague idea, or see just a hint of what might be. So the backbone supporting what you want to do is the *sincere desire to change*. The status quo has its own inertia, its own gravitational field. What you decide to do must be compelling enough to generate the energy necessary to break free of the opposing forces. For some, this is an epic struggle; for others it seems to come naturally. Do you embrace change easily? Is it a battle to believe your dream is worth fighting for? What elements were present the last time you made a significant change in your life? Did you initiate the change or did others? Can you feel the energy in your gut that will be necessary to overcome the status quo?

You may have made changes in your life that did not turn out well. You thought you had a good idea and an exciting plan for you life, but you crashed and burned—the kind of experience that might make you apprehensive about initiating another life change. If this is true for you, you will want to remember to take care of yourself during the change process (self-maintenance) and engage in activities that give you a sense of peace about what you are doing (self-renewal). In fact, when we begin to talk about writing your plan later in the book, be sure to include self-maintenance and self-renewal activities as an integral part of your plan.

It is good to reflect on why you want to make a change and move in a new direction, empowering yourself to make a decision that is right for you. I can think of three reasons you might want to make a significant change in your life/career. The first would be circumstances beyond your control that force you to make a change, even if you hadn't planned one. Secondly, you may want to change because you are unhappy with the way your life/career is working out. Thirdly, you simply want to improve you life/career by making positive changes that will lead to greater fulfillment. The *why* has to be more than passive discontentment. You need an irresistible desire to create new momentum for yourself.

CHAPTER 4:

The Magic Is You

Now you have warmed up by completing the assessment exercises, you have decided *what* you want to pursue, *why* you want to pursue it and *it is time to act*. Many people make it to this point, completing the work in Chapters 2 and 3 (Dream It/Learn It), and then…

they…

stop.

Perhaps feeling they did not get it right the first time, they find another book or process and repeat the work, but they get no farther because the next step is very challenging. What about you? Do you have sufficient information and the will to move forward? Are you ready to transform your dream into reality? You may not feel like you have everything you need to take the next step; in fact, you probably don't. You may think that nothing short of magic will get you through this transition. But I know that you can find the resources you need to proceed, and I say *The Magic Is You*.

Consider Niki, who was looking for a new job. She felt she knew who she was and basically what she wanted to do. She worked at a college managing a program for disadvantaged students. She had also worked as a writer. She liked higher education and wanted to stay in the field or at least in a field closely related to higher education—perhaps anywhere in the field of education, although she did not want to be a classroom teacher.

Niki did the normal things one might do when thinking about changing jobs. She saw herself working on the East Coast (she had moved out west) where the pace of life was much more suitable for her. She worked on a resume with a career counselor in the school where she worked. She watched the ads and submitted her resume several times, but with very little result. She did some more research and found other sources of job leads. Things were moving very slowly on the new job front.

One day she was talking to her boss, a college dean, about her desire and her boss said she would help her. (Remember, you never know where the resource will come from that will move you forward.) By approaching her boss, she made a much greater commitment to actually making a move than ever before. Up to this point, she was planning, but not stepping out to take significant action. Her boss made Niki rewrite her resume in an academic style known as a curriculum vita, and encouraged her to list all the accomplishments in her entire academic and work life. Her boss said she would be looking for opportunities for Niki to apply to appropriate jobs around the country. Her boss became her ally, her mentor, and a significant resource. Soon Niki was contacted for a telephone interview for a job in the Philadelphia area, an area ideal for her plan.

I have found that people can have very different reasons for wanting to change jobs. For many people, like Niki, it is to live in a certain part of the country or world for that matter. For others, it is the job itself, no matter where it is located. Still others want to be near friends and family or want to change jobs so their children can attend a better school. Whatever reason you may have for wanting to make the change, it must be sufficient to move you from planning and learning to actually taking action. *Taking action is the most critical move in the whole process.*

If the move from dreaming and learning about it to doing it is most critical, then how are you going to make that move? Again, I say *The Magic Is You.*

No power on heaven or earth can force you to make that move. *You* must be willing to do it. I know that fear and apprehension may get in your way, and I know that you may not be a big risk taker. That's O.K. You just have to decide you are going to do *something*. In Alan Laiken's "How to Get Control of Your Time and Your Life," he suggests you use what he calls the Swiss cheese method. You just bite off a little bit at a time until your task begins to look like Swiss cheese with all the little holes in it. Those little holes represent your active efforts. From dreaming and learning to doing. It's your choice: What will it be? A lifetime of dreaming and planning, a great leap of faith, or a steady, consistent, nibbling effort to act on your dreams? Mental preparation will be as important as anything else you will do to set your dream in motion.

I strongly urge you to include mental preparation in the visualization of your success. See yourself facing obstacles and overcoming them. You may be able to recall a time in your life when you were down and refused to be beaten or a moment when you overcame fear and acted courageously. Try to remember the feeling of triumph when you succeeded, and it will help sustain you as you activate your dream. This memory can be anything you have done in your entire life that made you feel good about yourself. The feeling of achieving is the energy you can use to power your new dreams.

If you will yourself to do something, especially something you have prepared yourself for, it will happen approximately the way you planned for it to happen. You will face fear, even terror. You may be too paralyzed to act. You may wish to avoid the risk. But you can't do what you want to do unless you decide to take a risk and find the will to change. If you will take the risk, your plan can move forward.

I have an idea that I think will help. Right now I want you to think about moving from dreaming and learning to doing. To make this transition as easy as possible for you, I want you to think of one small, easily achievable thing you can do *today* to move yourself from thinking about doing something to actually doing it. Do something that moves you an inch or two down your chosen pathway. It is important to write it down and to take action to complete this first item within 24 hours. Please complete the following exercise.

EXERCISE: ACTIVATING YOUR PLAN

Within the next 24 hours I will (describe specifically what you will do)

_____

_____

_____

_____

With these results:

_____

_____

_____

_____

By doing this, I have just activated my new life/career adventure.

The Magic Is You, explained

Why do I say "The Magic Is You"? Well, where else could the magic be? Why do you think the world is filled philosophies, theories, and ideas about how to fulfill your human potential? Why are there so many books in so many languages urging you to use one system or another to achieve personal success? Why do others try to persuade you to their particular way of thinking about life and its meaning? The answer may be that these ideas suit the author or lecturer, have worked for many other people, and allow proponents to influence others. Is that not what I am trying to do? Am I not trying to influence you to think about your life/career in a certain way?

Of course I am—but I am doing it with the recognition that if you don't buy my message, I am not going to help you change anything. I am not promising you anything, because I can't. Only if you act on my ideas can I be a factor in shaping your life. I believe the ideas and methods in this book will be beneficial for many people, but not all. I have no power to make you do what I suggest. That power rests solely and completely with you.

It is very difficult to do the things I am asking you to do. They may be the most difficult actions you will ever take. Doing this work is not easy. Some people search for a lifetime and never find real meaning for themselves. I have had three careers in my life: salesman, manager, and career counselor. Each one had appealing qualities that I enjoyed. I relish many aspects of my current career as a career counselor—but not every day and not in all ways. But after all's said and done, I love it far more than it ever bothers me. Every life/career has some parts that are enjoyable and some that are just drudgery. I have not yet found the perfect life/career where every day is sunshine and roses, but I am getting closer to my dream.

Getting you closer to your dream is my goal in this work. But only you have the power to make your own dreams come true— THE MAGIC IS YOU!

CHAPTER 5:

Creative Resource Development

*B*y now you have a better sense of who you are, what you value, what dreams you want to reach, and what mountains you want to climb. At the very least you should have an idea of the direction you want your life/career to go. Sometimes we do not receive a crystal-clear message about our direction, but something more like a hint. In the process of pursuing the hint, clarity often emerges. Assuming you either know for sure or have at least a sense of your direction, the next question is how are you going to proceed? Doing some research and finding the resources you will need to get started is your next step in the learning process.

Remember Susan and her soap-making adventure? Susan had to create many different resources to get her soap-making business off the ground. Many a business has been started in this way. If the business is successful, it will grow. If it is unsuccessful, then Susan can move on to some other endeavor, knowing that she gave soap making her best effort.

The Value of Failure

Remember, nothing is a success or a failure in an absolute sense,
because we always learn something in the doing. We learn more about
ourselves and how we handle either success or failure. It is said
that failure paves the path to success. If we don't try, we have
no chance of succeeding or failing. How big is the risk? Here is
a difficult question: Is it any riskier to try and not succeed or to
not try and always wonder about or yearn for what you never
attempted? Are you content to leave your fate in the hands of
others and let them decide your risk level?

Whatever it is you are trying to do, resources are out there that will
move you closer to it. Sometimes you might have to create the resource
yourself because the exact thing you need does not yet exist. However,
if you move in the direction of your dream, things that you cannot see
now will open up to you in an almost magical way. The magic comes
from you and the effort you put forth in manifesting your idea. Remember: *The Magic Is You.* When you direct your energy toward any idea of
something you are trying to do, and if you do it in a determined way,
your idea or your plan will be fulfilled or will lead to new opportunities.
The trick in this life is not how to make it happen; *it is in knowing what
you want to have happen.* Once you know what you want, you will be
ready to seek it out.

If You Want It, You Can Get It

How many times have you known or heard about a person who had
a burning desire to do something? Someone who was determined to
attend a school like Harvard or Yale or who wanted to become a doctor or a lawyer or a professional singer or dancer? The person was
absolutely consumed with the desire to accomplish his or her goal. Did
you ever realize how many were successful in accomplishing what they

set out to do? Did you ever wonder where they got the money and/or opportunities to succeed?

Almost all dreams are possible, once you make up your mind to do something, to create the resources necessary to carry out your plan. A living decision that drives you forward on a daily basis is a very strong motivator. Many, many people understand the concept of creative resource development and use it repeatedly; others may not understand the concept but use it without realizing it. The concept itself is timeless.

Creative Resource Development

I will give you an example as it unfolded in my own life, many years ago. I started college right out of high school and finally graduated fourteen years later; only fourteen years to get a four-year degree. But if I had not used the techniques of Creative Resource Development, I might still be working on my degree.

Let me tell you my story. When I graduated from high school, I was offered a scholarship to go to an in-state university. This is an example of Creative Resource Development that was done for me by my mother.

My mother, rest her soul, was severely afflicted with rheumatoid arthritis from the time I have any recollection of her. She was bed-ridden most of the time. But she had an active mind and great faith that things would work out all right. She knew if I was going to be able to attend college, I would need some financial assistance. So she took it upon herself, always believing she would succeed, to write to various colleges and universities and apply for scholarships on my behalf. I was a fairly good student in high school and there certainly was a financial need in my family, but I believe it was her energy and enthusiastic belief that she would get what she went after that ultimately made the difference.

As it turned out, I was offered not one, but three scholarships from three different schools. Eventually, I accepted the scholarship from a university in the state where we lived.

My first year in college was a total disaster. I accept total blame for my failure. If I had known then what I know now about setting goals and resource planning, the results might have been different—but I didn't and they weren't. In my freshman year I managed to lose my scholarship, lose my job (which was part of the scholarship), borrow money from my parents who could barely afford it, and ended the year with a stunning "C" average.

I was devastated! I had let *everyone* down: my parents, particularly my mother, the school, the scholarship committee and, most of all, myself. I did not return to college the next year. In fact, I did not return to school for two years, when I enrolled at another university on the other side of the state. I attended classes on and off for the next three years.

About that time I went to work for a state-managed public employment agency financed by the federal government. Because of the job, I was selected to attend a seminar at the University of Southern California (USC), where I picked up some additional college credits in public administration. So in eleven years altogether, I had acquired exactly one-half of the credits I needed to obtain my college degree.

Something remarkable happened to me at that USC seminar. One of our assignments was to go into the Los Angeles community and evaluate available social services. For my project, I decided to role-play an unemployed man who had just arrived in town. I went to the closest public employment office and asked a young man, Charley, for assistance. I said I needed a job and a place to stay.

I really didn't expect much would happen; yet Charley surprised me. Hearing my needs, Charley gave me two referrals to temporary jobs that were hiring immediately. In addition, he suggested a decent low-rent motel in the area that had weekly rates, and finally, he told where to be at five o'clock in the evening if I needed a hot meal. Charley was the definition of caring, effective public service. He went well beyond what I might reasonably have expected to happen. Talk about creative resource development!

I felt a little guilty as I left Charley's office, with a handful of referrals to take care of all my immediate needs—because I was just role playing. I didn't have the heart to tell Charley that I was completing a class assignment for the seminar. I have always remembered Charley and his commitment to serve the public in an exceptional manner.

I also worked in public service, but I felt I did not meet the standard set by Charley. After years of procrastinating, I made a decision at the USC seminar to complete my degree. Charley inspired me to try harder. I further decided that I was going to do it without giving up my job (I actually took on an extra job), and without any direct expense to me or my family. I resolved that I would spend only a minimum amount of time on campus attending formal classes because I simply would not have the time. Above all, I determined that my educational endeavors would relate to my current job and have practical value when completed. *I set a goal and directed all my energy toward its accomplishment.*

By the time I made my decision, I had been promoted to assistant manager in a new location. By merest coincidence, the location of my new job happened to be the home of a regional university. I inquired of the training branch of my employer whether or not they would like to send me to school to finish my B.A. degree. The agency training officer at the time was a marvelous man, to whom I will be forever grateful. He informed me that there was no money immediately available, but he would look around and see what he could do.

In a few days he called back and said if I wanted to take some classes that would contribute directly to my job performance, the department could pay for them. He added, somewhat deviously, if I found enough classes of this kind to constitute full-time enrollment, then I could take other classes because the cost would not increase. Once you have met the minimum number of hours to be considered a full-time student, most colleges charge you nothing more in tuition if you take additional classes.

I was delighted! Of course there were still some significant obstacles to overcome, but I could see a thin shaft of light pierce the dark unknown. The next thing I did was contact the chairman of the sociology department at the university and explained to him my desire to complete college, but that I must hold actual class attendance to a low level.

Once again, I had found the right man to create the right resource. This man, who epitomizes the true spirit of education, gave me *carte blanche* permission to deal with any of the professors in his department and work out learning contracts to satisfy course requirements. I want to emphasize the significance of this decision. First of all, "learning contracts" were not yet in vogue; this was a new concept that was just then being developed. Secondly, what made him decide my situation and learning contracts were compatible? I call the answer Creative Resource Development.

Learning contracts are formalized to a much greater extent now than they were at that time. A learning contract, in my case, turned out to be whatever I could negotiate with individual professors to satisfy them that I had acquired a useful body of knowledge in a specific area of study. I must admit to feeling some of the professors thought I was a little "off" when I told them I wanted to take some of their courses, but I did not want to attend classes. However, because I had the backing of the department chairman, I was able to work out satisfactory arrangements in most cases.

During this process, I frequently visualized in my mind what I hoped to accomplish. I would close my eyes and picture myself crossing a stage in a cap and gown receiving my diploma. If you picture yourself in a situation where you have already accomplished your goal, your mind releases and directs positive energy that empowers success. I found this exercise to be an immeasurable help.

In the next two years, I concentrated my thoughts and energy on completing my education, and I finally received my diploma. It took me 12 years to complete the first two years of college and 21 months to complete the last two.

I do not want to oversimplify my story. It was not easy to be persistent enough to succeed. Remember, I was working full-time in a demanding job. I had also picked up a part-time job administering civil service tests every other Saturday because I needed a little extra money for incidental school expenses. I was also supporting a family. Because I could not attend class, I had to do a mountain of research and write extensive project papers to meet the course requirements of the college.

The discipline was good for me. I was forced to become efficient in my use of time and to plan activities far in advance. I learned to engage my brain on short notice and in varied circumstances.

I tell this story to illustrate that you can create resources to meet your needs (created by your desire to do something) by seeking them, tracking them, synthesizing them and combining them. It is truly amazing how resources show up at just the right time, just when you need them. There is a Zen saying that goes: When the student is ready, the teacher will appear. My version is: When the resource is needed, it will be created.

I sometimes think of Creative Resource Development as a "life vector." In its simplest terms, a vector is a physical quantity with both velocity and direction. A common example of a vector is a particular path to be followed by an airplane. It is meant to guide the aircraft in a certain direction at a certain speed. If the airplane stays on the proper vector, it will reach its destination safe and on time.

Creative Resource Development is a way for you to set a vector, a life vector that will lead you to the correct resource at exactly the right time. Mind you, you must initiate the action by determining which vector will get you to where you want to go. But we have already spent the first few chapters of this book helping you identify desirable destinations. Your job is to pick the place you want to go, set your vector to get there, and the necessary resources will be developed out of the energy of your effort.

To put it in terms of mountain climbing, you determine where you want to climb on the mountain, plot your compass heading, estimate your speed, and propel yourself up the mountain. You will, of course, have tried to anticipate what you need to bring with you to support your effort. However, in mountain climbing, as in life, you cannot anticipate everything. You will need to find and create additional resources as you progress. It really is part of the fun of climbing that you cannot prepare for every eventuality and that you must create solutions to problems as they occur, usually by combining the resources of what you have in your backpack with what is available from the natural surroundings of the mountain.

You might be surprised to learn that Creative Resource Development is something you have already done in your own life. I have left some space below for you to write a description of a time you created a needed resource when there was none in sight. Perhaps you needed tuition for school, or some money to buy a car, or school clothes for the kids and you found a way to create those needed resources—but this is your story, so let me get out of your way.

I had always wanted/needed _____but in order to accomplish/obtain this I created a needed resource in my life at just the right time:

_____

_____

_____

_____

_____

_____

_____

_____

_____

Voila! If you needed proof to believe the theory of Creative Resource Development, you just provided it for yourself by writing about your own experience. Nothing is more convincing to us than our own experience. If you were unable to think of an example to write down, you can complete this exercise later.

I shared my story and asked you to write your own story briefly to emphasize the practicality of what I am proposing. The only magic in Creative Resource Development is the energy and commitment you put into locating what you need in order to reach your dream; the life vector you choose to follow. I want you, right now, to think of a something you will need in the near future. It can be any element of your dream or any other resource you would like to develop. Think about the following questions and write in your answers:

Can I specifically identify the resource I am seeking? (Write it down)

_____

_____

_____

_____

_____

_____

_____

Can I imagine ways to immediately begin to pursue this resource?

_____

_____

_____

_____

_____

_____

Can I improvise, if necessary, to adapt a resource to my need? How?

_____

_____

_____

_____

_____

_____

_____

Can I tell, for sure, when my resource need has been met?

_____

_____

_____

_____

_____

_____

_____

_____

If you can answer each of those questions in the affirmative, then you have the formula for successful resource development. We will be using the process of Creative Resource Development extensively as we move deeper into the processes in this book. However, if you accept nothing more than the efficacy of using a positive approach to create resources you need or want, you will have gained a valuable life asset. Here's the formula:

Idea + Belief + Pursuit = Creative Resource Development

CHAPTER 6:

Work It: Moving from What/Why to *How*

The first five chapters of this book have dealt with knowing yourself, reflecting on what you want in your life/career, why you want to change, finding the correct resources, and acting on your own behalf. It is now time to address *how* you are going to implement an action plan. The discussion has been mostly philosophical so far, but we will now get to the specifics of accomplishing the dream you are pursuing. What we need is a detailed plan. Now don't worry; it will not be hard to do *and* you will feel much better after you have done it. You probably will need a plan eventually to obtain financing from a lending institution or to present yourself to a new employer, so developing a detailed plan now will give you a head start.

People often avoid the planning process because planning, as practiced in most business and management circles, can be a long and complicated affair that chases its own tail. It can become more obstruction than action. Many spend their entire life just planning, never doing. Sometimes when a big company publishes a plan for the year, or the decade, it immediately goes on a shelf in the library and is rarely thought of or talked about. I want to help you create a plan that is yours, done in *your* style, that reflects your thinking, and that is simple enough to be written on one or two pages. The plan should be helpful in terms of direction, but not so restrictive that you cannot accommodate reasonable variations. Some consultants think a plan like this is obsolete the minute it is written because business conditions change so rapidly. I believe that if the plan is written as a general guide, states the underlying principles that support the plan, and provides specific goals for specific periods of time, it will be used and useful.

So how are you going to write a plan? Such planning is not just for people who want to start a business, project or activity that is solely dependant on their own efforts. If you prefer to work for others as an employee or as a volunteer, the planning process is every bit as relevant for you. Your life/career path may be a unique combination of working for others and doing your own thing. These ideas are not mutually exclusive; you can do either or both. I believe that *you* are in control here and can manage your life/career with great flexibility.

You have this great idea; this dream and you have committed yourself to making it come true. How do you do that—specifically? It is quite simple. Just complete the following exercise and you will have a plan. You may wish to make it fancier or more detailed, but it's not required. You *must*, however, complete the exercise. *Try it*—it will be fun and you will feel wonderful about jumping this significant hurdle. Do not worry about making a perfect document. The whole idea of this exercise to get something concrete down in writing so you can see your whole plan in one complete package. Let's begin..... .

Exercise: My Dream (II)

The planning system I am proposing—Dream It, Learn It, Work It—is based on continuing to use the methods I have presented throughout the book. Simply stated, Dream It means finding the life/career you *want* to pursue. In other words, *your* dream. Learn It is preparing yourself to fulfill your dream of choice; learning what you have to learn, creating the resources you will need, choosing the path you will follow and developing the logistical support you will need to be successful. Finally, Work It simply means to begin moving in the direction of your dream. You have found your dream, you have prepared yourself as best you can and now you must begin the journey. And it requires courage.

To the best of your ability, just fill in the labeled spaces and complete this draft of your plan.

DREAM IT

Your Dream: In Chapters 1 & 2, you thought about who you are and what kind of a dream you have about your life/career. Even if you didn't write it down at that time, see if you can describe your life/career dream in a few words. Keep it simple, keep it focused, and see yourself in it:

_____

_____

_____

_____

_____

_____

_____

_____

I am going to do each exercise I am asking you to do, so you will have a model to follow if you are having trouble getting started.

My "Dream It":

My dream is located where I help people succeed in their lives/careers. The immediate manifestation of my dream is to write and publish a book that synthesizes what I know about helping people (including myself) experience success, as they define success for themselves. I also see myself conducting seminars and giving lectures to large groups of people who are interested in further exploring the ideas contained in my book.

Learn It: Find Your Resources

Your "Learn It": What will you need to learn and experience in order to prepare yourself to complete your dream? This part is not doing it, but researching what you need to do to get ready. This is learning what you need to learn and creating appropriate resources. This is the work we did in Chapter 3.

_____

_____

_____

_____

_____

_____

_____

_____

My "Learn It":

Since I have never written a book before, I have many things to learn. I do have confidence in my ability to write clearly and share my thoughts and ideas. I will find books about writing books and I will follow what seem to be the best suggestions. I will begin to write immediately because I must learn to organize my message. I will ask others to edit my material because I know good writing usually goes through several drafts. When the time is right, I will seek advice on how to get published, but if I am unsuccessful at that, I will explore self-publication. I may take a class in non-fiction writing. Ultimately, I know that writers must write. My primary approach to writing a book will be to write and write and write and trust I can fit my writings into a book at the appropriate time. When the book is completed, I will begin to develop workshops and lectures based on my book and research methods of marketing them.

WORK IT: TAKE ACTION

Your "Work It": This is where you take the leap of faith from describing your dream and learning how to manifest it to actually beginning to do it; from dreaming to reality. It is the moment of truth. It is when you need the courage and the energy to start moving down your chosen path. It is the time when you look up at the mountain and feel a little fear about how far you must go. It is having your *dream* well defined, having begun to acquire the learning and resources you will need, and *now* taking the first few steps towards manifesting it. Some people live in Dream It and Learn It land most, if not all, of their lives. They have many reasons to explain why they can't Work It. But without Work It, the dream is just a dream and the learning is just learning without action. It's as if you have all your gear in the car to go on vacation, but never start the car to begin the trip.

In the movie *Grumpy Old Men,* one character says: "The only things we regret in life are the risks we didn't take." Writing a Work It plan makes it seem more manageable. And yes, I am trying to encourage you because you cannot realize your dream from where you are now sitting or standing.

Let me suggest an easy way to write the Work It list. Think of five things you could do, right away, to begin taking action. What can you do to get started? Do not worry about the order in which to do them, just get five action items or goals on the page and your first plan will be complete.

1. _____

2. _____

3. _____

4. _____

5. _____

My "Work It":

1. I will write either in my writer's notebook or on the computer a minimum of three days per week for at least two hours per day.

2. I will read and research the mechanics of writing and publishing a book.

3. I will find editors who will critique my drafts.

4. I will research and survey sources that I wish to draw from and/or quote in my book.

5. I will design workshops and lectures based on the material in my book and test them out on various audiences.

Done and Done

Congratulations to us both. If you just completed this exercise you have taken a huge step forward. If you have not completed this section, but want to finish reading the book before you commit yourself, no problem. You must, at some time, complete this step. However, you can do it in your own way or you can follow the model I have provided. The most important thing is to get something written about the three sections of the plan: Dream It, Learn It, Work It.

CHAPTER 7:

Action Planning

I cannot stress enough that the completion of your Work It list is critically important to what you will do next. It's difficult to go forward without that crucial step. Chapter 6 gives you the big outline or plan for your life project, small business, occupational change or advancement, family or volunteer activity. I believe it will give you a sense of direction. Random ideas have been put in order and listed as logical steps to take as you move toward fulfillment of your dream. Next, choose any one of the five items on your Work It list to work on in greater depth. Please choose only one to do, as it will force you to decide what's most important for you to be doing right now.

Multitasking

I suggest you work on only one item from your Work It list at a time. Most of us can only work effectively on one thing at a time anyway. You may think you can multi-task and work on all five items simultaneously and if you can successfully do that, more power to you. For the rest of us, myself included, we lose too much concentration if we scatter our efforts too widely. Can you relate to this in your own life? Is it better to do one thing well and thoroughly and be done with it, or to do 14 things adequately or poorly and have to deal with them over and over again?

The Work It list is a consolidation of the actions you can take to make the Dream It and Learn It statements come true. I am asking you to choose the most important item on your Work It list and write a few specific action steps you can take to complete the item. These steps should be actions that you can complete and then cross off your list. Measurable progress is about as motivational as it gets. When you can check off an item, you realize you are one step closer to completing the item. You are one step further up the mountain trail.

Give it a try. I will provide a process you can use to write your action steps. I will give you models to look at and use. Remember *The Magic Is You*, and *only you*, so in every instance in this book where I ask you to do something, feel free to do it your own way: just make sure you do it. I strongly urge you do it in writing because there is something very clarifying in writing out your plan.

All you have to do is fill in the blanks and watch the plan systematically unfold. First, go back to Chapter 6 and transfer your Work It list to this section. If you didn't complete the Work It list before, now might be a good time to return to it. Or you can just read on and finish the exercises later.

Work It List

1. _____

2. _____

3. _____

4. _____

5. _____

Exercise: Action Planning

First, choose one item from your Work It list. Choose the item you want to work on first. Choose an item that can be completed in a reasonable period of time so you achieve an early victory.

THE WORK IT ITEM I WILL PURSUE IS:

_____

_____

_____

_____

FIRST ACTION STEP: (Format: I will do (what)_____
with whom (could be just yourself)_____
by when _____ with this expected result_____.)

WHAT?_____

WITH WHOM?_____

BY WHEN?_____

EXPECTED RESULT?_____

SECOND ACTION STEP: (Same format as above)

WHAT?_____

WITH WHOM?_____

BY WHEN?_____

EXPECTED RESULT?_____

THIRD ACTION STEP:

WHAT?_____

WITH WHOM?_____

BY WHEN?_____

EXPECTED RESULT?_____

FOURTH ACTION STEP:

WHAT?_____

WITH WHOM?_____

BY WHEN?_____

EXPECTED RESULT?_____

FIFTH ACTION STEP:

WHAT?_____

WITH WHOM?_____

BY WHEN?_____

EXPECTED RESULT?_____

Now it's time to work on completing the five action steps.* Or you may want to finish reading this chapter, but then be sure to return to these action steps and complete them!

Remember Niki, the job seeker who wants to move to Philadelphia? Let's assume that she wants to make a good life/career move that will get her closer to her dream. Briefly stated her dream is to work in the field of education in an administrative capacity. She wants to be in charge of a program or a work area and she wants to be able to both supervise her staff and provide some of the direct service to students. All of this in Philadelphia.

Her Work It list challenges are to write a good resume or curriculum vitae, learn about the market for her services in Philadelphia, practice job interviewing, network with knowledgeable contacts in the area, and study ways to commit herself to making this all happen.

The first item on her Work It list she wants to pursue is to understand the market for jobs in Philadelphia and in the process make useful contacts in the area. Here is her Action Planning strategy:

ACTION PLANNING

FIRST ACTION STEP: (WHAT, WITH WHOM)) I will identify all educational institutions in the greater Philadelphia area. I will set-up and maintain data files for each institution including size, location, total number of employees, number of employees who do work that appeals to me, administrative structure, hiring process, growth potential for the institution, cost of living, housing availability, social/cultural life, and "fit for me." (BY WHEN) I will complete this action within 60 days. (EXPECTED RESULT) I will have a much better sense of the labor market in Philadelphia.

---

*You may ask why there are five action steps, and not six or four for that matter. Five is just an arbitrary number that works well for me. If you only need three action steps or if you need 10 action steps, no problem.

SECOND ACTION STEP: (WHAT) I will make contact with a least (WITH WHOM) one person in each institution who can give me a sense of potential career opportunities. (Although I am primarily interested in permanent, full-time employment, if it is the practice of a certain school to hire staff on a temporary basis and then convert them to career jobs, I may consider that option.) (BY WHEN) I will maintain these contacts primarily by telephone and e-mail as soon as the FIRST ACTION STEP is completed. (EXPECTED RESULT) I expect to make and maintain several useful employment contacts.

THIRD ACTION STEP: (WHAT) I will contact (WITH WHOM) all the people I know in the area, all the important people in my life, and let them know that I am committed to making this move and seek their advice and assistance (BY WHEN) at the same time I am working on the SECOND ACTION STEP. (EXPECTED RESULT) I know that in the doing of this, I will further commit myself to my plan. I will be putting myself on the spot to make the move, to find the job, to be in control of my own life.

FOURTH ACTION STEP: (WHAT, WITH WHOM) I will (BY WHEN) immediately begin to monitor job opportunities in a variety of ways. I will find appropriate web sites for job searching, check publications such as the Chronicle for Higher Education, monitor local newspaper ads, watch business news for new opportunities in the institutions I am monitoring. (EXPECTED RESULT) I will find a number of suitable job openings.

FIFTH ACTION STEP: (WHAT, WITH WHOM) I will maintain a positive attitude about making this move, visualize myself living and working in the Philadelphia area, imagine myself working energetically in my "perfect job." (BY WHEN) Beginning tomorrow I will devote a minimum of 2 hours per week in completing ACTION STEPS 1 - 5 which will (EXPECTED RESULT) land me a job in Philadelphia within six months.

That's one example of how action planning works. Remember that form is not the most important thing; commitment to get it done is. Writing down your Action Plan forces you to think through your choices and clarify your own thoughts. Sometimes, if you write down your action planning steps, you'll realize that your heart is not in it and it turns out to be rather a fanciful thought instead of a dream you can truly get energized and excited about. An Action Plan can be challenging to complete, but should not be made so difficult that you'll never get it done. If you write an Action Plan that is not quite perfect, use it as a first draft and begin to act on it. You can always come back later and perfect your plan. There are two words in this section of equal importance, Plan and Action. Both are needed and important, for either one without the other probably will not work. The Plan is a map of where you're going; the Action is your effort to get there. Without a Plan, your energy may send you in the wrong direction, and without Action the best map on earth will not get you closer to your dream.

My Action Plan: I will now share my action plan regarding the number one item on my Work It list: I will write either in my writer's notebook or on the computer (or both) a minimum of three days per week for at least two hours per day.

I must say this is getting a little stressful, because I am writing these words in mid-February, the time I normally start my income tax preparation. This reminds me that any Action Plan must be flexible enough to allow you to complete other important activities when necessary. I will confess to you that right now I do not know how my Action Plan will come out regarding the first item on my Work It list. It's O.K. A part of the magic of action planning is that the writing of the plan requires you to commit to one course of action or another. Let's see how mine turns out.

FIRST ACTION STEP: I will write for two hours, either in my writer's notebook or on the computer where I am producing my first draft or a combination of both, on Monday morning (or Monday evening as long as my wife is taking a class Monday), Tuesday morning, and Wednesday morning. If I miss a day of writing, I will make it up on Thursday morning. If I write all three days as planned, I can use Thursday A.M. as a bonus day for the week. I will not use the weekends to do any serious writing, because I will use them to enjoy my life and to work on special projects.

SECOND ACTION STEP: I will maintain a log, in my writer's notebook, of the amount of time I write each day to be sure I am meeting the goal of six hours per week. If I am not meeting the standard I set for myself, I will reexamine the FIRST ACTION STEP and make the necessary adjustments. If writing is to become an important part of my life, I must maintain a certain discipline about doing it.

THIRD ACTION STEP: I will spend at least one additional hour per week reading my notes in the writer's notebook and/or reading and editing the material in the individual chapters I have written so far. It seems especially important to review the writer's notebook on a regular basis because what I write in the notebook tends to be free form and of the moment. Some of my best thoughts come to me that way. I will record this additional hour of review in my time log (see SECOND ACTION STEP).

FOURTH ACTION STEP: I will continue with steps one, two and three until I have completed a first draft manuscript of the entire book. I will continue to dedicate the same amount of time to this project after the first draft is completed, but I will undoubtedly alter the way I use the time. I will complete my first draft of this book by July 28, my birthday.

FIFTH ACTION STEP: I will move on the next item on my Work It list.

Quick Review

Have you written or are you writing your Action Plan? I hope so, because in the system I am proposing to you, writing the Action Plan is important. This is where you've really got to buckle down and state exactly what you are going to do—right now—to get your own project up and running, to start filling your dream balloon with helium. Thinking about action planning is interesting, and may work to a limited extent. In the long run, however, I think you'll be much better off if you put it in writing. As I've noted before, the act of writing down the words is a commitment in and of itself. This is the final step in the Dream It, Learn It, Work It process and represents the payoff for all the hard work you have done so far. Once your Action Plan is completed, you're on your way. Rev up the engines, squeal the tires, and take off en route to your self-defined success!

CHAPTER 8:

More Creative Resource Development

*N*ow that you have an Action Plan, you need to actually begin working on it. It is time to step out smartly in the direction of your dream. You will need to develop some resources to get your first Work It item completed. I say develop because I am going to propose a process for you to use that is a proven winner when it comes to resource development.

When I was a young man, I worked for the state employment agency in Washington State. I did reasonably well and was eventually offered the job of manager of the employment office in the city of Aberdeen.

I met two other people who were involved in social services in Aberdeen. One man, Duane, was the director of a community action agency (created during the federal government's War on Poverty in the 1960's). The other man, Ralph, was the administrator of the local welfare office. It turned out that all three of us were appointed to our respective positions at about the same time. Since we were all in the business of human services, we soon became acquainted and later friends as well as business partners.

One day while we were having lunch together, we decided that we should form a not-for-profit organization to provide professional services in Grays Harbor County, strictly outside of our regular jobs. Though not knowing much about how to form a non-profit corporation, we proceeded with great enthusiasm. Duane did the research, I helped write the incorporation papers, Ralph contributed ideas and the corporation was created and duly registered.

This is another example of Creative Resource Development. In fact, we named our corporation, Resource Management Services. We started with an idea (dream), learned what we needed to learn about what we needed to do, followed through and created the corporation. However, we really did not have a good idea of what we could do within the structure of the corporation to create income. We thought we might provide some kind of management training or deliver other services.

We finally decided to take advantage of Ralph's cooking skills. We knew that the county had built a racetrack for cars at the fair grounds *and* they were looking for concessionaires. There were two venues: one large venue serving the general race-going public and a smaller venue serving the pit crews and race car drivers. Against all odds we were chosen for the smaller venue. Mind you, we did not have one piece of the needed restaurant equipment, and very little money in the corporate bank account.

So Ralph and I began the quest to find the equipment: things like hooded stoves used in commercial kitchens, a large refrigerator with a freezing unit, a double sink to meet health department requirements, food worker permits, vendors to supply needed food and beverage items, and enough of everything to be able to open our concession on the first day of racing. Adding to our money worries was the fact that in the concession business, you pay for everything as it is delivered. Right away we had a cash flow problem. We needed to be open for the first day of racing so we could sell all our food and drink and generate enough cash to restock for the second day of racing. It was tight, but we made it.

We had to take in more money than we were spending, because re-stocking the concession booth was a weekly exercise. In order to do this, we decided we needed more customers. Only a limited number of people were permitted in the pit area, but if we could sell to all or most of them, we felt we could make a profit.

Ralph was experimenting with a new hamburger he called a Chicago Burger. It was really an onion burger with all the trimmings. People flocked to our booth when we were cooking Chicago Burgers—we wondered why. Finally, it dawned on us that cooking onions sent a sweet, almost irresistible, smell wafting out into the pit crew area activating salivary glands with Pavlovian efficiency. From then on, whether he was cooking Chicago Burgers or not, Ralph always had a batch of onions frying on the grill, guaranteeing we had a steady stream of customers, generating a healthy profit.

A few months later, sitting around in the same restaurant/bar, we decided we liked the idea of management training because it would give us credibility as management professionals. We decided we would teach an introductory class in supervision and management at the local community college. However, the college did not know we had made this decision, and we had no reasonable expectation to believe they might want us to teach such a class. But we all believed that if you have a specific idea of something you want to do and if you begin to move in the direction of making that idea come true, amazing and wonderful things will happen to allow you to do what you are committed to doing. Let's say that we believed there is energy in the universe that responds when positive energy is expended on a direct vector—the Life Vector mentioned in Chapter 5. I cannot prove this theory; I just know from my own experience and the experience of others that it works.

Some say the response comes from their idea of God, others might say it results from some exotic mathematical theory such as Chaos, still others say it is just good old American ingenuity, and some say it floats in the wind and hides in the clouds. I do know this: If you use this process it will work for you. As long as you move in the direction of your dreams, they will come true in one form or another. In fact, I'll bet that if you review your own life just a little bit, you will be able to identify times in your own life when you were trying to do something that was very important to you and it seemed impossible. But you just kept pushing and suddenly the whole world opened up and the right resource appeared at the right time to allow you to do what you desperately wanted to do. Take a moment to reflect on this idea and validate my theory from your own experiences. What have you created in your own life out of your *desire* to make it happen?

While you ponder this, let's get back to my story. We were sitting around in the restaurant with a big idea but no clue as to how to proceed. We decided we could write a prospectus for the class, find someone at the college who had the authority to fund such a class, and see what happened—we had developed an action plan. Ralph and I prepared the document and met with the Academic Dean. He said the college did have an interest, we could offer a class, and he would be glad to have us. Just that easy. Oh, there was one *small* caveat. If we did not attract a minimum number of students, students who would pay enough tuition to cover the expenses of the college and pay us a stipend for teaching the class, then the deal was off. So what do you think? Did we teach the class or not? Well, of course we did. Moreover, the class was such a success that we created an advanced class for the next academic quarter and taught it, too.

I tell you these stories to encourage you to get out there and start working on your Action Plan. And even when you cannot see any possible way to make something happen, something that needs to happen in order for you to move forward, just keep pushing. There is a way. You may encounter obstacles. You may get in your own way from time to time. You'll bump into barriers you must climb, go under or around to find a way to keep moving ahead. Be persistent. Remember that positive energy on a direct vector will create positive results.

I have one more story to tell you in this chapter. It's about a woman I worked with in my capacity as a career counselor. She was a single mother, with one child. She had been working at the local Head Start program for a number of years. However, she felt she was dead-ended on her job because she did not have a college degree. That's why she was talking to me in the first place.

We engaged in a process of career counseling, including assessment testing (finding out who you are and what you might want to do in your life/career) and she discovered that she ultimately wanted to be a fulltime Yoga instructor, something she did on a very part-time basis in her own home. I asked her what it would take to begin working in that direction. She said she would have to have a place to give the classes, she would have to advertise for people to take the classes, and she would have to be able to work it into her college class schedule.

I said, "Well, why don't you just do that now?" As I recall, she said, "I never thought of being able to do it right away, but you're right and I am going to get started. I am excited." Needless to say, she moved in that direction created the resources she needed to move forward and now has both a college degree and a full-time career as a yoga instructor. It doesn't get any better than that. The yoga instructor is the perfect example of Marsha Sinetar's famous book, titled "Do What You Love and the Money Will Follow." This is why it is very important to complete your first Action Item, the one you committed to do in Chapter 6 and made a plan for in Chapter 7. So get started. Right now!

CHAPTER 9:

Maintaining Momentum

Congratulations! You're in the process of completing your Work It list. (You *are* working on it, right?) Well, let's say you have four more Work It items before you complete your overall goal. When you completely finish item 1 on your Work It list, you are at least one-fifth of the way done toward realizing your dream. You have come to a crossroad and need to make a decision about which direction to go next. You are 20% complete, which means you have 80% to go. But let's think about this for just a minute. It could be, and often is, that the first Work It item is the most challenging and often the most time consuming. In my case, if I don't write on a regular basis and produce a first draft of this book, the other steps really don't matter.

I attended a seminar by Bill Onken, author of "Managing Management's Time," at which he said more than once that everything takes longer than it takes. He also said everything costs more than it costs. His point, in both cases, is that you cannot ever know everything about what is going to happen as you proceed in your quest. Getting a start and moving ahead is the best you can do most of the time. How long your project will take or how much it will cost can only be estimated.

I am saying, in a way, that the 20% is more important than the 80% because it is where you are starting. How many projects, good projects, in your life have been lost for lack of a starting place? Furthermore, the

80% may not take as long as the 20% because you have already gotten things rolling at a good pace. I do not need to find an editor if I do not have a draft. I don't need a publisher, if I don't have a book. The question I address in this chapter is how do we start and finish fulfilling our dream?

I strongly suggest that you complete the Work It list in the order it is written. You can go back to Chapter 6, write down the remaining items and complete the same process for each Work It item, as you did for the first one. Take item 1, complete it. Go back and pick up item 2, complete it. Keep doing this until every item on your Work It list is checked off, completing your entire sequence. You have accomplished or are accomplishing a major dream you've had in your life. Naturally, you could dream new dreams and start the process all over, but that is not what this book is all about. It's about settling on one dream, doing the necessary planning to bring your dream to fruition, and working the plan until your dream stands before you and the whole world to see. It means looking down from a high place and surveying your dream kingdom.

If you look at your Work It list, you will see that even after you have completed several items on your list, there is more to do. As you reach the later items on the list, they will tend to be items that may keep you busy for longer periods of time—possibly years. Stick with your number one dream and work towards its refinement for as long as you can generate sufficient positive energy to remain actively engaged. Continuing to manage that which you have created may keep you busy for several years if everything goes the way you plan it. For instance, once this book has been published, I intend to market it in various ways for a considerable period of time.

On the other hand, you might get tired of your dream project in two or three years and abandon it to pursue other interests. You won't know until you get there. Your life could change considerably in two or three years.

The commitment of your time and energy toward the accomplishment of your dream requires discipline. There will likely be interruptions and detours along the way. Many things may not go exactly as you planned them. The discipline of spending a certain amount of time working on your project each day or week will make you a better time manager. The time spent will move you closer to your dream, even if you start off on the wrong foot and have to retreat and regroup. It is all part of the learning the process—learning what works for you. Discipline and commitment will keep you moving when you want to quit, when it's dark, when you can't see the finish line. Accomplishing your dream may be the most difficult thing you have ever done in your life, but the rewards will justify the effort.

A few years ago, when I made a commitment to return to school and obtain a higher-level academic degree, it took me forever to find a school that taught what I wanted to learn, when I wanted to learn it. Furthermore, when I first applied to this school, I did not hear anything from them for almost a year. I thought they had rejected my application because I was too old, or because I had been out of school too long. It seemed to me that the least they could do was send me a letter turning down my application.

Just when I was ready to give up my dream, I thought about it some more and began to get a little angry. I decided I was going to see someone in authority at the school and find out why they didn't accept me. When I did, the school could not even find my application. It turned out that there had been a change in administration in the program I was applying for and the paper work had been lost in the shuffle. The school was very apologetic, invited me to resubmit my materials, and I was soon accepted into the program.

I had been very close to giving up. Had my dream not been strong, or had I not followed up, there would have been a dark ending to this story and I would have an empty feeling of failure. That's why I encourage you to stick with your dream, climb your mountain, work your plan and don't give up too quickly because *the resources you need are out there* —they might just be temporarily hiding from you.

A practical tool to assist you in the development of your project is a format, similar to the one in Chapter 7, that will allow you to complete all the items on your Work It list and decide roughly how you are going to do them. When you complete the item you are currently working on, you can just come back to this chapter and pick up the next item. By the time you do that, you may want to revise your original Action Plan, so I will leave you some extra room.

Let's say you have completed item 1 on your Work It list. *The first thing you do is celebrate.* In the next chapter I will strongly suggest taking the time to celebrate small/large victories along the way, at the time they occur. Next, since you have created and completed an Action Plan, you are ready for item 2. Just plug and play using the format listed below and you are ready to move on. On the other hand, if you do not want to wait until you have completed item 1 before you do an Action Plan for the balance of your list, this would be a good time to complete it.

EXERCISE: ACTION PLANS FOR YOUR NEXT WORK IT ITEMS

The Work It list item I will pursue next is:

_____

_____

_____

_____

_____

_____

_____

_____

FIRST ACTION STEP: *(Format: I will do (what)_____ with whom (could be just yourself)_____ by when _____ with this expected result_____.)*

WHAT?_____

WITH WHOM?_____

BY WHEN?_____

EXPECTED RESULT?_____

SECOND ACTION STEP: (Same format as above)

WHAT?_____

WITH WHOM?_____

BY WHEN?_____

EXPECTED RESULT?_____

THIRD ACTION STEP:

WHAT?_____

WITH WHOM?_____

BY WHEN?_____

EXPECTED RESULT?_____

FOURTH ACTION STEP:

WHAT?_____

WITH WHOM?_____

BY WHEN?_____

EXPECTED RESULT?_____

FIFTH ACTION STEP:

WHAT?_____

WITH WHOM?_____

BY WHEN?_____

EXPECTED RESULT?_____

NOTE: Just copy the last two pages as many times as necessary to write an Action Plan for all the items on your Work It list.

You might wonder why I gave you all of these formats to complete. It is not because I think my format is vastly superior to any format you might invent for yourself. Quite the contrary. If I stimulate you to write your own format for any of these exercises, great! I would be delighted.

Some people like a lot of detail; some people just want the broad strokes. The planning formats I have given you are somewhere in the middle.

Once you master the cycle of completing action steps one after another, it will become a habit. Once it becomes a habit, you will do it automatically without much conscious thought. This is a good discipline to develop as a habit, because it can be applied to any area of your life. It does not inhibit spontaneity, it actually frees you up to operate very spontaneously because you have the assurance that your dream is on track and your important action steps are being completed in a regular and creative manner.

You may not stop to do these exercises after you finish your first Action Item. You may be so wrapped up in the completion of your first item you never slow down long enough to come back and really plan the next item. Most of us do work that is assigned to us for some purpose such as earning college credits, or meeting a requirement at work, or to get ready for some recreational activity. We do what others require us to do. But I hope you will view these assignments a little bit differently. Remember: You are responsible for yourself, and nobody else can do this work for you. Here is the question: If you gave yourself the assignment to do all this work, would it be as important to you as if your boss gave you the assignment? I certainly hope so, because when you take yourself more seriously than other people who influence your life, you are beginning to make *you* the priority in reshaping your life. If you are going to be responsible for your own life, then here is a place where you can begin to take control of your destiny.

Acting in a way that may seem selfish, at least for a while, is probably what you're going to have to do. Selfish in the sense that you will not be put off in striving to manifest your dream through your own efforts. You will need the self-sufficiency required to generate power to complete your dream tasks. The pats on the back you will receive along the way will come from your own hand, most likely, especially in the beginning when you are the only true believer in your vision. So when the going gets tough, just pick up a mirror and give yourself a pep talk. Works every time.

CHAPTER 10:

Maintaining Perspective

Where are we? Are you losing steam or are you filled with more energy around your project than ever before? Does it seem that what you are doing is silly and simple and that no one will be interested in it when you are done? Do you feel you have been successful so far because you have been doing most of the work yourself and you have not had to share very much about it with others? Do you fear rejection when you do begin to share? Do you have doubts about why you ever started this thing in the first place? Are you ready to quit? Are you in a slump?

Maybe you are in a slump because you are looking not so much at where you have been, but how far you still have to go. This is to be expected. Recently, I read that the designated hitter for a professional baseball team felt he needed at least 70 at-bats during the pre-season to get his swing just right. Imagine that. He has been playing baseball for years and it takes him over 200 swings under game conditions to feel he is ready to play the season.

So after the season starts, and he has found his swing again (or it came back from vacation), you would think he might hit the ball almost every time he steps up to the plate. You might think he could never have a slump in hitting because he regained his swing, his timing, and his baseball vision. You would be wrong. Every hitter in major league baseball goes through a slump period almost every year. They all have games where they get no hits. Sometimes the slumps come after they have enjoyed a considerable amount of success. A really good hitter in baseball is one who has a .300 batting average—that's just three hits for every 10 at-bats. If you are successful in your venture at least 30% of the time, perhaps you are more successful than you realize.

Do professional baseball players quit coming to bat even though they are in a slump? Absolutely not. They keep on swinging until they hit themselves out of the slump. Therein lies the message for all of us. If the professionals can survive a slump, why can't you? Don't be too hard on yourself if, after you complete item 1 on your Work It list, you crash and burn for a while. The message to all of us is to keep on swinging, even when we are hitting poorly, or not at all. In the process of designing your life/career, you must be in it for the long haul. People will start a project and just at the point where they might begin to enjoy some success, they drop it and start a new project. Film director and comedian Woody Allen maintains that 80% of success is just showing up. I am suggesting to you that 100% of your chances at success in your life/career lies in your ability to hang in there and keep on swinging.

At the college where I work, my boss conducts job-finding sessions with students and alumni who are seeking full-time paid employment. She uses a model for the sessions called Job Club. Job Club is a system developed by Nathan Azrin, who believes job finding is a numbers game. Participants in Job Club are given data that suggests it takes, on average, 25 employer contacts to land a job interview and 10 interviews to receive a job offer. Just think of all the rejection an average job seeker must face. However, if you consider each rejection a stepping-stone on the way to 25 employer contacts, and eventually 10 job interviews, you can maintain a more positive frame of mind during the job-hunting process. Temporary failure at any point along the way toward reaching for your dream can be viewed as valuable experience that will payoff for you in the long run. Attitude can be everything. How you see things will be the way you experience them.

Although the principles outlined in this book are universal, some people may have to work harder than others to attain their dreams. If you are a member of the mainstream culture where you live, your path may be easier. If you are superbly educated, you may get off to a quicker start. If you live in an affluent area, you may have more opportunity for material gain. But everyone encounters obstacles in life. If yours are greater than mine, then stick with the program until you even the odds. What I am encouraging you to do is not easy, not for anyone, privileged or not; I am just saying it is possible regardless of your circumstances. Many people have overcome seemingly impossible odds to achieve their dream, to climb their mountain, to succeed in life. You can, too.

Reading this book may be part of your education, but doing the activities recommended in the book provides the experience. Reflect on your success. Think about all the hard work that went into completing item 1. Remember how impossible you thought it was going to be to get it done. Be thankful for all the support you received along the way from family, friends, contacts, fellow travelers and rogues.

Yes, *rogues*. The people who tell you that you're wasting your time, that your idea is no good, that 50 other people have tried that idea and it didn't work then and it isn't going to work now. Ya gotta just love those people! Why? Because they are the type of people who will stir up your spirit and deepen your resolve. If you can't handle a rogue or two, your commitment may not be strong enough. As I've said *The Magic Is You* and no one can take that from you. So trust yourself, trust your most valued relationships, and smile at the rogues and understand the depth of their inadequacy. Don't let them project their feelings of failure and disappointment on you. Unfortunately, for every person who will cheer you on and encourage you, five or more will think you're nuts. Listen to the positive voices and take the negative voices in stride. If you maintain this perspective, you will develop a resilient spirit.

Ominous Abundance

I was hiking with my wife near Mt. Rainier in the fall, heading up the trail from Reflection Lakes to Paradise Glacier. The trail was well maintained, but fairly steep. It was a beautiful day, but a little on the chilly side. Fog filled many of the dips and valleys as we moved up the trail. About halfway to our hiking destination I spotted a rock outcropping and on this rock was one the largest chipmunks I have ever seen. Fat and happy, without a care in the world, he apparently lived in an ecosystem that favored him greatly.

Neither my wife nor I had a camera, so the moment was filmed only in our minds. We continued on to Paradise Glacier. After we had some lunch, we began to climb down the trail to retrieve our car. When we got to the rock outcropping, I thought I might see the chipmunk again. Instead, on the very same rock, we saw a huge black raven sitting where the chipmunk had been. It was a thrilling sight. The raven sitting on the rock, looking out over the fog filled valley below him. I felt a little chill. I thought of Edgar Allen Poe. We watched the raven for several minutes, and then started down the trail again, passing within a few feet of this brooding bird. He never moved and paid us no attention.

I felt fortunate to have seen such a magnificent display of nature, both coming up the trail, and now, heading back. We proceeded for another mile or so when I thought I saw something in the trail. I beckoned for my wife to come and look. We waited a few seconds and then we both saw a large deer on the trail. He had not yet seen us, but we were enjoying seeing him. Suddenly, he lifted his head. He was a four-point buck and he appeared to be in velvet. He was just grazing his way up the trail, eating the foliage as he went.

Finally, he saw us and I assumed he would run away, so we proceeded to move down the trail again. Surprise! He not only did not run away, he looked directly at us and began to move up the trail he must have thought was his very own. We backed up very slowly because we didn't want to scare him and, well, because we were a little scared ourselves at his boldness. So we danced for a while. He would move up, we would back up. He would graze, we would edge forward. Eventually, he spied some delicacy on the hillside that ran beside the trail. He eased himself up the hillside, never in a hurry, and continued his feast. We froze and hoped he would stay in view so we could watch him some more. He moved slowly on his way and when we could no longer see him, we proceeded down the trail once again.

What a treat we had received that day. First the chipmunk, then the raven, and finally the deer. All of a sudden these words flashed in my mind: Ominous Abundance. I thought about what those words might mean. I decided it probably meant that the earth is an abundant resource and takes very good care of its creatures—the plump chipmunk and the handsome buck. The raven and the fog made me think we cannot always see very far in front of ourselves, we cannot predict the future and we never know who might be watching. Part of the message in the word "ominous" is a warning that abundance for us will exist only as long as we do not abuse it. I was reminded that everything we experience in life carries some risk. Sometimes we are aware of the risks, but many times we are not. It was a profound moment in my life; one I will never forget.

Knowing abundance is possible, but that achieving abundance should be accompanied by a sense of balance in using available resources, leads us into thinking about what to do next. Once again, knowing who you uniquely are and how you can best make your own life meaningful is the key to running the life/career race. So how will you get started on your next Work It item? Are you so excited that you have already begun? Are you suffering a letdown from all the effort you put forth in completing item 1? What will it take to get you up and running, running until you've completed your entire Work It list? You will not have completed your first sequence of Dream It, Learn It, Work It until your entire Work It list is checked off and complete.

Some people just fall into an ideal situation, allowing them to begin climbing their mountain with all the resources they need to get started; most of us are not so lucky. We have to hunt and scratch to get a start on our dream. Movie director Steven Spielberg once said that there were not enough days left in his life to tell all the stories he wanted to tell. His dream, in a way, is telling stories about other people's dreams. Spielberg got his start in high school by making home movies about things that interested him. When he was ready to attend college he was rejected by the acclaimed UCLA Film School because in high school he spent more time making films than studying for his classes. Instead, he went to Long Beach State. Yet that didn't seem to slow him down in becoming a world-famous director. The phenomenon of rejected college applicants succeeding in spite of their disappointment has been dubbed the 'Spielberg Effect' by Stacy Berg Dale and Alan Krueger.

It is amazing how the world opens up to you when you are focused on pursuing a dream. Resources appear at just the time they are needed. You receive help from unexpected sources. You find the money you need to get started. And just when it seems all is lost, you get what you need. And if you don't, you have learned a hard lesson and you will do it more successfully the next time around. I mean you can't lose. Where else in your life can you receive a guarantee that you cannot fail, especially if you believe that each setback is a stepping-stone to success. How can you lose? I encourage you to keep at it and expect positive results.

In the foreword of their book "In Search of Excellence," authors Peters and Waterman say that in order to achieve excellence in your business you must have dedicated employees who buy into your dream. They say you don't have to tell workers what to do in detail if they know what you are trying to do in general. You are the manager of your own life/career. Get yourself moving in the right direction, and you will pick up many allies along the way. Loyal people who help you keep on track.

Or think of your life/career as a foot race. You have decided you want to enter the foot race and compete against others for the winning prize. You envision yourself crossing the finish line at the head of the pack: you Dream It. Next you begin to train for the foot race because you know little about what it takes to run the race. You consult with experts by reading what they have written and by talking to them in person whenever possible. You start running and experience the pain of using neglected muscles, tendons and bones. You run very short distances in the beginning because it is all you can do. As you begin to get in shape, you run faster and farther. Soon you are able to run the same distance you will have to run in the foot race: you Learn It.

Finally, the day of the race is here. You have done everything you can prepare, but you have not yet run the race. You are ready to Work It. The moment is now. How you fare in your first foot race is not very important. You may win the race, you may come in last place, or you may not even finish the race on that particular day. But you do run the race. You give it a shot. You overcome your fear and step up to the starting line. You start running when the starter's gun fired and you run. How glorious is that? You *run the race and sooner or later you learn to win the race, which is your ultimate goal.* How much more can any of us do: dream about running our race, learn about running our race, and actually running our race and winning. This three-step formula can be repeated endlessly on any life/career venture you may choose.

CHAPTER 11:

Celebrate!
The Power of Ritual

What will you do when you complete item 1 on your Work It list? Will you immediately begin work on the next item? A temptation in our busy world is to say, "Whew! I'm glad that's done. What's next?" But it is a mistake to miss opportunities to celebrate your victories in life. To others they may seem like small victories, but you are the one who won them and you have a right to be proud and happy. Besides, how much do others know about the real effort it took on your part to reach your goal? How many times did you feel discouraged and want to quit? How many times did the rest of your life interfere with your direction? And how many nights did you wake up thinking about your goal and wondering if your chase would ever end and how much energy it takes every single day just to keep it going? So in completing your first Work It item you are *winning*, and it's time to dance!

There are many events in our lives that come with pre-packaged rituals and celebrations: births and birthdays, marriage, school graduations, holidays, retirement, etc. They are sustained in our culture because they serve an important function. First of all, celebrations signal the significance of the event and the rituals allow us to experience a sense of closure so we can move on with our lives.

I am suggesting many more celebrations to motivate and inspire you as you strive to realize your dream. Celebrations are a way to mark milestones on your journey. When you complete an item on your Work It list, celebrate! When you complete a significant step in your Action Plan, celebrate! Give yourself the recognition you deserve for sticking with your plan and completing it. Do not wait until you have achieved all of your goals, stop along the road and have some fun. Make it a habit to celebrate.

Celebrating small victories along the way is one way to sustain your journey. If what you are attempting to do with your life were easy to do, you probably would have already done it. Recognizing the struggles you are likely to face makes it imperative that you have release valves to reduce pressure; ways to maintain your perspective about what you are trying to do. In sustaining yourself and the effort required to complete your Action Plan, you can periodically reflect on what you have already accomplished and celebrate the battles already won.

Although celebrations of victories, large and small, are important, they alone will not be enough. It is a very good idea to develop a network of people who will support your efforts—in fact, including others in your celebrations is a good idea. You may also need a mentor or life coach. Someone who can act as a sounding board for ideas, who can make helpful suggestions, and most importantly, someone who has your best interests at heart.

Most things do not come to you wrapped up in a neat little package. When you complete something important in your life, do what you need to do to bring closure to the event. It may or may not be a formal celebration, but you can create a ritual or a small ceremony of your own to mark the event as important. I hope I will never miss another opportunity to celebrate an important happening in my life. So when you complete your first Action Plan, or even when you complete a significant step within your Action Plan, take time to celebrate.

Reward Yourself!

Several years ago, I attended a two-day stress management seminar. At the end of the first day, the instructor asked all of us to write down some little thing we wanted to do for ourselves that we had put off as not being important enough. He suggested doing something for yourself, in a seemingly selfish way, as a great stress reliever because you were saying to yourself that you were important enough to spoil.

I took the assignment seriously and went to the store and bought myself two leather belts; belts I had been needing (at least in my mind) for quite some time. It just never seemed to be the right time, and they cost more money that I wanted to spend on myself and it did seem selfish to me. The feeling of actually buying the belts, out of my own wants, was liberating. I don't know when I felt so good about doing something just for myself. Of course, I realized later that is was easier for me to do it because the instructor of the class had given me permission to do it; he assigned me to do it.

To my surprise, when we came to class the next day, the instructor did not even ask the class if they had completed their homework assignment. I suspect he knew that most people in the class would not complete the assignment—too busy, so much else to do, I'll do it later, I don't really deserve it, etc. I, on the other hand, was eager to share my experience. It bothered me a little that I never got a chance to share with my classmates. However, that in no way diminished the value I received.

I still have those two belts, rather worn by now, but I love wearing them and when I do, I am always reminded of the day I did something special for me. If you had been in the class, would you have completed the homework assignment? How long will you wait before you give yourself permission to do something nice for yourself? When is the last time you did something special for yourself? My suggestion is to quit reading this book, right now, and go do something nice for yourself. Get a massage, a manicure/pedicure, go to the zoo *without* the family, purchase a small accessory, visit a museum or gallery you've been wanting to see, sneak off to the movies, buy a personal diary, sign up for piano lessons. Just remember that whatever you choose must be *by you, for you.*

Perhaps the most likely place for people to miss the opportunity to celebrate is at work. People dedicate their working lives to the completion of difficult projects and then barely stop long enough to cheer. It is the responsibility of conscientious managers to make sure that a job well done is rewarded. Although there may be monetary rewards, such as a bonus or a raise, this is not the celebration that counts the most. The joint celebration of a team of workers (most work is done in teams these days) who all went above and beyond the call of duty to do something better than anyone could have imagined is what really counts.

The last project I worked on as the human resource director for a public employment agency lasted about four years. The purpose of the project was to design and implement a new job classification system for middle managers. It was a huge change from a traditional civil service system, to a system more like what you might find in private business.

It was a gut-wrenching process. We not only had to design the rules for the new system, we had to design and implement a whole new system of compensation. The nature of the project, since it affected every division in the agency, required high levels of coordination and cooperation. Not only that, we had to convince the workers who were to be directly impacted that the project would be to their benefit. Even if they did not gain salary as a result, there would be more potential for them in the future. The team I was working with pulled off this massive reorganization of the personnel system with very few hitches. When the new system was implemented, no appeals of the decisions were made regarding classification or salary. As a result, the team and I were recognized for the work we had done—in a very formal, understated way.

But I wanted to shout it from the rooftops! I wanted to have a debriefing of the process. I wanted to celebrate. But alas, it did not happen. Every time I think about the project, I feel proud of the work we did and how smoothly we implemented this very complicated new system. And as I am writing about it now, I realize it is one of the projects I need to write down on my own list for celebration and completion. These things can slip by so quickly; they are gone before you know it. But until they are officially closed (you are the only one who can do that), they are not yet complete.

I read a story about the 3M Company a few years ago and they not only celebrated their successes in a big way, they celebrated their failures. If they had financed a research project to discover or improve something, and if at the end of the project-funding period they had not accomplished their goal, they brought closure in a dramatic way. The way I remember the story, they would bring the team together and fire off a cannon. Symbolically, it blew the old project out the door, recognized the good effort of all involved, and effectively released the researchers from the old project and got them ready for a new one. What a fabulous idea. Celebrate victory, celebrate defeat, celebrate everything. When the celebration is over, and only when the celebration is over, move on!

CHAPTER 12:

The See-Saw of Life

Let's project our lives into the future. In a sense we do that anyway by creating our own futures with our present actions. So here we go…

In this scenario, you have just completed all aspects of your first dream, with the exception of the effort you must make to maintain it. You have started the soap business, or landed the job in Philadelphia, or been promoted on your present job, or written your book, or written and sung your own song. Your dream has materialized into a real thing you can touch and feel and enjoy. Soon after you began to experience more success in your life than you had ever imagined possible, you started to think about the issue of life balance.

You did not yet believe your own success and knew failure was just around the corner if you slowed down and took care of your personal needs for even a minute. It felt like being on a treadmill where the reward for going around and around is that you get to go around and around some more. You were a little burned out and wondered if all this success was what it was cracked up to be. Although you were successful, beyond your wildest dreams, you couldn't stand it and you were waiting for the bubble to burst. You knew something was missing.

What was missing was you. You wondered if your life was out of balance.

You reminded yourself that *The Magic Is You* and that you could apply the magic to any area of your life. If you did it once, you could do it again even if the first dream bubble did burst. So what was there to fear? Nothing.

The happy ending to your projected future is that you did everything you needed to, became a happier (more content) person, and gained control in those areas of your life you considered to be most important. Celebrate when this future actually materializes for you.

EXERCISE: LIFE BALANCING

The following exercise will allow you to judge for yourself where you stand in the life balancing process. Just rate your sense of satisfaction with your life in each of the six areas listed below;

(1 is not satisfied at all and 10 is completely satisfied.)

EMPLOYMENT

1   2   3   4   5   6   7   8   9   10

LOVE

1   2   3   4   5   6   7   8   9   10

MONEY

1   2   3   4   5   6   7   8   9   10

RECREATION

1   2   3   4   5   6   7   8   9   10

FITNESS

1   2   3   4   5   6   7   8   9   10

SECURITY

1   2   3   4   5   6   7   8   9   10

Take a few minutes to reflect on the results of this exercise. Are you reasonably well satisfied in all areas? Are one or two of the areas dominating your life to the exclusion of others? Are you happy with how your life is balanced at the moment? Is there a move you could make to achieve more satisfaction in one or more areas?

Write your thoughts about the satisfaction/balance in your life here:

_____

_____

_____

_____

_____

_____

_____

_____

Whatever thoughts or ideas occur to you while writing this exercise can be used as guidance as you continue your Action Planning. Including life-balancing activities in your Work It list will be a reminder of the importance of considering your whole life as you move towards your dream. No matter what else you are doing in your life, these issues remain a constant for all of us. If life were a gyroscope you would have to keep it spinning all the time or run the risk of toppling over. So how are you going to keep the spin in your life? And if you should topple from time to time, as we all do, how are you going to get your life gyroscope spinning again—and forever?

The Recreation Scene

Paula was exhausted from a difficult week at work. Filling prescriptions may not look like difficult work, but it is. Paula is on her feet all day, she is talking to unhappy customers and over-worked doctors, her supply order is inevitably short of one thing or another, and since she is one of only two pharmacists in the store, she often works well beyond her scheduled hours. She is making good money but she is not enjoying it much. She got married three years ago to a physician's assistant who works an equally frenetic job. Paula and her husband have no children, but might some day after they are financially secure, own their own home, and have time to raise them properly.

Paula's chance to recreate comes on the weekends she is not working, when she and her husband both have time off. Paula likes to go a small spa in the nearby mountains where she and her husband can relax and enjoy themselves.

Paula made the reservations several weeks earlier in hopes that every-thing would work out and they would be able to go. When they arrived at the spa, they checked in and then went directly to the hot tub for a soak. Paula then scheduled a massage and an herbal wrap. When she arrived in the treatment room, soft classical music was playing in the background. First the massage, gentle but firm, began to loosen all the tension in her body. She became so relaxed she dropped off to sleep sometime during the treatment. She was gently awakened a few minutes after the massage was completed and in came the girl to do the herbal wrap. More relax-ation, more sense of cleansing her body, mind and soul.

When she returned to her cabin, her husband, who had gone for a swim in the heated pool, poured some wine and they listened to the soft music that was piped into their room and took a short nap. After they napped, they became romantic in a relaxed, unhurried way. It felt so good to be held by her husband and not have a thing to think about. She remembered why she had fallen in love with and married this won-derful man.

A quaint but elegant dining room at the spa is where they went for dinner later that evening. A little more wine, a shared chateaubriand,

and a dessert of fresh strawberries dipped in hot chocolate warmed in the fondue pot. Paula was more relaxed that she had been for the last six months. She wondered if this weekend could last forever. She and her husband strolled around on the trails in the cool evening air before returning to their cabin. They watched a romantic movie in the room and went to bed early. Tomorrow they were going horseback riding with a small group of guests also staying at the spa.

They woke up early in the morning, snuggled for about an hour, took a shower, and got dressed for the day. As she was dressing, Paula realized that they had more romance this weekend than they had in the previous month. It was wonderful to reconnect with her husband, but she knew something was missing.

The horseback riding was exciting and more daring than she had imagined. Her horse was a little frisky and some of the trails were quite narrow. It was exhilarating to say the least. Her husband was more of a horseman and gently kidded her about her daring adventure. But tonight was the last night of the mini-vacation and Paula began to dread going to work on Monday morning. She wondered why it took a weekend away to reestablish her relationship with her husband and with herself, for that matter. She began to brood about it and became tense.

When her husband approached her in a loving way that night, she was not in the mood and rejected his advances. He accepted her decision, but she could tell that his feelings were hurt and his ego slightly bruised. She slept in fits and starts that night. There was little conversation between them at their last breakfast of the weekend in the quaint but elegant dining room. The weekend was definitely over and Paula and her husband transitioned to the employment mode as they drove home that afternoon. Paula kept asking herself what had gone wrong. It had all been so right, and suddenly it all went bad. Was it her fault? Did her husband do something to irritate her? Her life was somehow out of balance, and her priorities were mixed up. What could she do?

Paula picked up a copy of "You ARE Your Career" and began to design changes in her life. She realized she couldn't always wait until the weekend to live her life and enjoy some recreation. With the cooperation of her husband, she cut back on her work hours and he established a more predictable schedule. They set aside one night per week where they had a party, any kind of a silly little party where the object was to be in touch with each other and enjoy the companionship that had been missing in their marriage. Paula joined a yoga group and got up early twice a week to attend classes. She also practiced yoga at home for at least one hour, three times a week before her husband got home. She began to reconsider her dream of becoming a compounding pharmacist and participating more directly in the patient healing process. She eventually changed her entire life, living out who she was and balancing all aspects of her life. She was happier, her husband was happier, and they both had a clearer idea of where they were going and how they were going to get there.

This story illustrates how ineffective the weekend getaway can be in the struggle to keep some fun loving, high-energy activity in your life. You must build recreation into your life as a priority, and when you do, the getaway weekends really do become all fun and games because you know you are returning to a pleasant, well thought-out life, not the chaos of employment domination. First the dream, then the learning, then the doing. The formula will work in all areas of your life. Since *The Magic Is You*, you can create the necessary resources to make your dreams come true. It isn't that most people can't make their dreams come true; they can. The problem occurs when you don't have a *well-developed dream* that *energizes* and *directs* your life.

The Root of All Evil

You guessed it; I'm going to address the issue of money. You are inundated with advertising from all media to buy the latest and greatest this or that. You receive mail, email, and flyers encouraging you to accept fabulous offers for new credit cards or refinancing schemes. These offers are sometimes very hard to resist. My thinking is that if you have a money plan for your life you'll be in a better position to fund *your own* dreams instead of being overly influenced by external forces.

Since I'm no expert in money matters, I'm going to recommend some words of wisdom written by professional money manager Karen Ramsey in her book "Everything You Know About Money Is Wrong." I don't intend to give you a big lesson on how to manage your money here; I just want to raise your awareness about some of the everyday problems and opportunities that involve money. Ramsey's book is based on practical advice. It is not a get rich quick scheme. Ramsey does a very nice job of suggesting solutions to many of the money issues you may be experiencing, which is why I commend her book to you.

Another book that deals especially well with the emotional aspects of money management is "The Financial Wisdom of Ebenezer Scrooge" by Klontz, Kahler, and Klontz. Although the title may sound a little unusual, I can assure you that it is an excellent book about transforming your relationship with money.

So there are two good resources about managing your money. Of course you can find many more by actively applying creative resource development to identify additional resources.

But something still might be missing…

What might be missing is the thrill you experienced when you manifested your first dream into a living, breathing, bucking reality. You had settled in and organized your life in a healthful way, but you knew it was time to move on. You either had to seek another promotion on your current job, or had to seek a new job, or needed to expand your business, or needed to return to school to complete what you needed to complete, or needed to volunteer for another organization, or needed to leave the rat race for a less frantic life style. I don't know what it will be for you, but I can assure you that it will be something. You must start dreaming again because dreaming is a way of life. A very rewarding way of life, even if it is a bit challenging.

This chapter is all about what the *next* dream is going to be. You have already proved to yourself that you can realize a new dream because you have already done it—or you will when you finish reading this book. Your dream can be anything you want it to be. The only difference between an immediately doable dream and a more challenging dream is the amount of time it takes to manifest it. You reapply the strategy of Dream It, Learn It, Work It and you move forward with the same enthusiasm you used the first time. You remind yourself that *The Magic Is You* and all things are possible. You renew your faith in the principle of Creative Resource Development and you begin again.

First you dream again. As I mentioned earlier in this book, most people fail at the dreaming level because they were somehow taught that dreaming is bad—sometimes life teaches that dreams never come true—that it is time to give up dreaming and go to work—that their dreams died the day their first child was born—that dreaming is a waste of time—that dreams without action amount to nothing—that dreaming eats into the precious 168 hours you have to spend each week—that dreams are fantasies not facts—etc., etc. etc.

Yet without dreams there is no hope and without hope there is nothing. Everything in this life started as an idea, a dream if you will. Sometimes the dreamers only dreamed and others created the reality. I am telling you that you can have it all. If you dare to dream, you dare to live. If you dare to live, you have a career. If you have a career, you have a purpose. If you have a purpose, you have direction. If you have direction, you have will. If you have the will, you will!

How many famous bands started in a garage somewhere? How many astronauts dreamed of going to outer space as a kid? How many athletes became professionals because they had a model to pattern themselves after? How many scientists were discovering stuff when they were young? Do you remember that Mozart was writing music at three years of age? Do you know that one of the Three Irish Tenors is a double amputee who has had three successful dreams he fulfilled: as a surgeon, as a para-athlete, and as a singer? How many people do you know who seemed to do the impossible? What about the guy down the street from where you live who had a crazy idea that everyone said would not work, but it did? What about the nerdy girl you went to school with who is now a renowned professor at a major university? How can we look at all these examples, both near and far away from our own lives, and not believe it is possible to create the life we want? I mean, really, the good life is just one dream after another.

So the challenge in your life, in your career, is to Dream, Learn, and Work, over and over again. Daring to dream and daring to live is a never-ending cycle.

In our culture we have a bias against dreaming. In fact, if when you were in school you said something about the big things you were going to accomplish in your life, you were probably teased and ridiculed about it. "Oh yeah, man. You're really going to be a rock star, star athlete, stand-up comedian, president, Nobel Prize winner, inventor, published writer, rich person, movie star." Or maybe you had another dream that others laughed at. It is interesting to note that the many books written by "experts" encouraging people to do a little more dreaming sell like hot cakes. I'm not knocking it because if there were no need, the books would not sell. I am only suggesting that dreaming isn't the hard part; how you go about realizing your dreams is.

EXERCISE: FIVE-MINUTE DREAM LIST

Let's have a dream session. Go find a piece of paper and a pencil and for the next five minutes write down all the dreams or aspirations you can think of that are of particular interest to you. They could be childhood dreams (some of which we never get over) or current dreams. Just write randomly as the ideas come to you. I know it is a little scary to write down a dream because you think it carries an obligation to act on it. Well, not in this exercise. This exercise is a "dream releaser." I want you to get in touch with the dreams you already have but have not acknowledged. I have done the same below.

My Five Minute Dream List

Climb Mt. Rainier

Become a full-time writer/facilitator

Learn to ski back country

Rent an office and hire some employees

Complete a PhD. program

Become financially independent

Create programs for senior citizens

Travel the world

Create a foundation and give charitably

Live by the sea

Help poor people become rich

Run a marathon

Be married forever

Compete in the senior games

Be a peace maker

Become a medical doctor (a childhood dream)

How difficult was it to do this exercise? If you wrote down just one dream, then the exercise is a success. I know that you have some dream in the back of your mind that has lain fallow for a long time. The point is to recognize your dreams, recognize you have them with you at all times, and recognize that they are pretty easy to access. Whether or not you act on them is another matter. Some you may want to activate, and others you may wish to admire and wonder "what if?"

Using the list you just created, I would like you to complete a Personal Growth Contract related to something on that list. The idea of a Personal Growth Contract is to make a commitment, a contractual commitment to yourself, to identify something you are going to do for yourself and to lay out a simple plan to do it. What you decide to do for yourself does not have to be a big thing but it does have to be significant to you.

I recall doing a Personal Growth Contract once where I contracted with myself to learn how to cross-country ski, something I had never done before. I encourage you to take the time to fill in the blanks on the Personal Growth Contract right now and see just how good it feels to commit to do something you have always wanted to do. The instructions are simple to follow, and this is a great exercise because it is easy to do: You are making a deal with yourself for yourself. It is a liberating experience. So relax and begin. It's fun!

EXERCISE: PERSONAL GROWTH CONTRACT

Personal Growth Contract

Fill in the blanks below and in a very few minutes you will have completed your first Personal Growth Contract.

DIMENSION: What dimension of your life would you like to change or impact as you write your contract: personal life, work life, love life, recreational life, spiritual life, etc? Write it down briefly.

_____

_____

_____

_____

_____

_____

_____

_____

ASSESSMENT: What is your assessment of the current situation and what would you like to change or improve in your life? Again, write it down.

_____

_____

_____

_____

_____

_____

_____

_____

GOAL: Exactly what do you want to accomplish? I suggest you set a goal you feel confident you can complete and you will benefit from a sense of success as you move forward. O.K. Write it down and mean it.

_____

_____

_____

_____

_____

_____

_____

OBJECTIVES: What are the small successes along the way that will let you know you are moving in the right direction; bite-sized accomplishments that will help you fulfill your goal? Write down two or three.

_____

_____

_____

_____

_____

_____

_____

STRATEGY: What methods will you employ to complete your first objective, second objective, and so on? What are the actual steps in the process you will use to complete each objective and ultimately your goal?

Step #1:

_____
_____
_____
_____

Step #2:

_____
_____
_____
_____

Step #3:

_____
_____
_____
_____

EVIDENCE OF GOAL ACCOMPLISHMENT: How will you know when you are done—when you have completed you goal to your own satisfaction?

_____
_____
_____
_____

TARGET DATE: By what date will you have completed your goal? Be specific.

_____
_____
_____
_____

Congratulations! Having just completed your first Personal Growth Contract, I hope you are anxious to begin work on it—you should do something tangible toward fulfilling that contract right away. If you do, you have chosen wisely. If you are not excited about your goal, you may need to re-think it and put some more of your personal energy into it so it has special meaning for you. This is a process you can use over and over again throughout your life. In my office, we do a new one every year.

If the idea in your Personal Growth Contract is large and potentially complicated, then I would recommend using the Dream It, Learn It, Work It system to do more detailed planning. If, however, your objective is something relatively clear and simple (like learning to ski), then the Personal Growth Contract works very well. The cycle of Dream, Learn, Work is self-correcting and can sustain you for a lifetime; the same can be said for a Personal Growth Contract. How long each cycle will last for you depends on you. Some people will go with their first dream and never need to do anything more than tweak it a little bit now and then. Others of you may be more restless and need to start a new dream adventure on a regular basis. The only rule I might suggest is to stick with your current dream project until you have reached manifestation before you move on. Many of you will want to keep Dream #1 going strong while commencing with Dream #2. It is all up to you because only you can know what you want to do—not what you should do, but what you *want* to do.

Lena and Stacia

I would like to share with you a real life example of how powerful a Personal Growth Contract can be. Lena, a single mother working as a program coordinator at a four-year college, was employed in the Career Development Center. Her boss, Wendy, had employees complete a Personal Growth Contract each year.

One year, Lena, who is creative and artistic, made a contract with herself to learn the floral business. She loved working with flowers and believed if she became qualified as a florist, she could not only buy her supplies wholesale, but that she might be able to prepare flowers for weddings and other special occasions. A little extra income would be helpful.

It was not easy, given her life responsibilities, to find a floral school and make the time to learn her new trade. Lena persisted, became qualified, and began to "flower" weddings. Her reputation grew and soon she had a thriving side business, in addition to her normal job.

Somewhere in this time period, Stacia was hired as a career counselor in the same office. She and Lena found out they had much in common and Stacia began to learn the flower business from Lena They both shared a dream of being in business for themselves. However, Stacia really wanted to manage a gift shop. The combination was one that had possibilities.

They researched business materials, wrote business plans, and generally developed a strategy about how they could go into business together. In the meantime, they were both now involved in the wedding business. They also computed how much money it would take to start their joint business and scouted for business locations.

I am not exactly sure how they found the money they were looking for, but they did. But it really doesn't make any difference how or where they got the money, because the process of Creative Resource Development predicts that the resource you need will show up when you need it—if you are prepared to receive it. Since their planning was detailed and complete, the moment they knew the money was available, they phased themselves out of their jobs at the college. They found an excellent storefront location in downtown Olympia and Newbury Bay, Ltd. was born.

Lena and Stacia have now been in business over two years. They are doing exactly what they planned to do: selling flowers and selling gifts. And in a big way, it all started because Lena created and completed a Personal Growth Contract.

Now you might ask, if the Personal Growth Contract worked so well for Lena, why shouldn't I just use it instead of the complete Dream It, Learn It, Work It system? Hey, that would be fine with me. The complete system is more structured and therefore may be easier for you to use. However, if the Personal Growth Contract is all you need to get started, good for you. I'm less concerned about how you get started and more concerned that you *do get started*. As always, the choice is yours—use the tools that work for you.

In the movie *Bruce Almighty* God suggests to Bruce that if he wants to see a dramatic change is his life he just has to realize that he, Bruce, already has the power to make it happen.

You are never, never, ever done producing/creating your own life/career. You're in the game of life for as long as you draw breath. There is always a dream to pursue. In a manner of speaking, this system is environmentally friendly because you recycle yourself over and over by transforming your natural materials into some new form. You are careering (living) the good life: the one you created.

CHAPTER 13:

Beyond Ourselves

The next step, as usual, is up to you. There is not much point in doing all the things I have suggested in this book if there is not some greater purpose to your work. The purpose may be to become rich, to travel the world endlessly, to serve your fellow humans, to provide for your family, to become highly educated, to seek knowledge and truth, to change the world, to stop pollution, to create peace in the world, to find your soul mate, to have children, to own a fleet of antique cars, to be an organic farmer, to be a steward of public lands, to help the less forunate, to defy large corporations, to create large corporations, to make music, to make love, to play sports at the highest level, to ride your bike around the world, to sail to England, to help others succeed, to write, to sing, to paint, to dance, to prance, to raise dogs or cats or cabbage, to cook food, to design houses and buildings, to fly in the sky, to ski full-time, to lead, to follow, to pray, to heal. Answer this question and you may gain some insight about your greater purpose:

If there were no limitations in your life,
what would you do?

Here's what one man did...

Patrick

Patrick is a man who has an interesting, if somewhat unusual life story. Briefly stated, Patrick completed high school in the 1940s and went to work in the logging industry around Bellingham, Washington. He worked as a logger for several years until one day he was applying for unemployment benefits and was offered a job as an unemployment claims processor. He worked for the state employment office in Bellingham for many years until he was promoted to a management position in Bremerton, where he eventually became the top manager in the office.

He joined the Washington National Guard somewhere along the way and spent one weekend a month as a non-commissioned officer in the Guard. He continued in the National Guard for over thirty years.

Finally, Patrick retired from both the employment office and the National Guard and could become a man of leisure. However, Patrick was civic minded and decided he wanted to do something to help the poor in his community. He realized that his hometown of Port Orchard had no thrift store where poor people could buy life essentials at a reasonable price. As he had a connection with the Catholic Church in Port Orchard, he inquired about the possibility of starting a St. Vincent DePaul Thrift Store in the area.

He was encouraged to put together a legal structure, including a board of directors, to begin the process. He was also told that there were no financial resources to assist him in the venture, but he could volunteer all the time and money he wanted to in order to get things started. That is exactly what Patrick did.

He and his board began to put the pieces in place to start the thrift store, but had to work out of borrowed space. Eventually, Patrick and the board earned and raised enough money to open a small storefront operation in an older section of Port Orchard. It was a risky venture, because they had to commit to a lease and they weren't sure they could make the payments. In this case I think it would be appropriate to say they literally took a "leap of faith."

The store produced income rather well considering the circumstances and Patrick was able to hire a professional manager to help him with the day-to-day challenges of operating a retail thrift store. His wife also pitched in and volunteered many hours of her time to make the store a success. It wasn't easy, but it was working because Patrick had a dream and he was manifesting that dream into reality.

The store moved and expanded and today Patrick has a staff of 8 to 10 fulltime workers, many of whom would probably not be employed if not for the store. The store also has many volunteers. The store provides job training for people who need to learn a new job. Furthermore, Patrick and his board have created a pool of money which they use to assist poor people in the community who have temporary needs for essentials such as housing, food and clothing.

Patrick worked for several years without compensation, until the board finally insisted he take a small salary. On more than one occasion, the store did not have sufficient funds to meet the payroll, and Patrick put up his own money to cover the funding gap.

Patrick, who is well into his seventies now, still goes to the store every day. He is the man in charge. His dream is about having a purpose in life greater than his own personal wants and needs, and appreciating the blessings in his life by giving back. Patrick is a marvelous example of Dream It, Learn It, Work It in behalf of others. The St. Vincent DePaul Thrift Store in Port Orchard, Washington exists today because of one man's dream and a lot help from his friends.

You see, an eternity of possibilities exists to guide you in your life/ career journey. But you must decide. Well, you really don't have to decide. You may not yet be ready to put your footprints in the sand. But if you are, I encourage you to decide on the larger purpose of your life. Once you do, everything I have suggested in this book will work in the direction of your overall life purpose. Richard Bolles of "What Color Is Your Parachute" fame refers to this process as finding your life mission. Management consultant and writer Steven Covey writes about people having a personal mission statement. Leadership guru Tom Peters says you need to know generally which way you want the herd to go. Purpose is about a general direction.

Getting beyond ourselves and finding a purpose greater than we could ever hope to accomplish in our lifetime is a constant motivator; there will always be more work to do. Age has nothing to do with it. People who grow old without a life purpose often die early. People who have accomplished everything they hoped for in life by the time they are forty years old have a real dilemma. Professional athletes, especially the so-called superstars, often seem to struggle with having once been the best at their sport and then trying to find a purpose anywhere as exciting or fulfilling after they retire. How will you find the overarching calling for your life? You are fortunate indeed if you already know the answer to this question.

I have a few suggestions. You can begin to write in a journal all the thoughts you have about your life purpose. If you get yourself into a relaxed state of mind before you begin writing, the words will come almost automatically. It is important to stay focused on the question of the day: What is the largest purpose of my life? If writing in a journal is not your cup of tea, then pick-up your fishing pole and go fishing by yourself and ask the fish, or the lake, or the sky, to give you some clues about your life/career mission. In any case, when it comes to you, try to write it down in some form or another so you can refer to it from time to time.

Another possibility is to talk it over with your spouse or significant other. Whether you realize it or not, the day-to-day decisions you make within your family unit may offer big clues about a jointly adopted mission. Something larger than life attracted you to each other; discover the essence of the attraction and you may make remarkable discoveries. I think it is best to write down your joint mission in one form or another—a poem, a family mission statement, a slogan, a phrase.

Those of you not so fortunate as to have identified and articulated a life purpose that will sustain you in whatever circumstance you may find yourself, might want to pause and reflect for a moment. Is this a good time for you to consider this weighty topic, or is it just too stressful right now? Is your philosophy based on a belief that the good times will roll forever? Are you able to cope? "What Should I Do With My Life?" by Po Bronson may be a helpful resource since he uses interviews with successful people to ferret out the principles of purpose. Help to find your life's purpose is out there for you, and you will probably find it in unexpected places.

One of the most uplifting things I heard recently was a radio show being broadcast from Qatar just after the start of our war with Iraq. The host was interviewing a longtime Kuwaiti citizen. He said his region was famous for having a fatalistic attitude about war and life. He did not seem overly stressed, he was going about his daily business, and he assumed that his life would be good because in his region they lived through four separate wars. He was concerned, but not anxious. He believed he would survive the whole thing because he had before. I found his attitude very reassuring because he totally accepted the idea that the war was beyond his control, or anyone's control for that matter, and the outcome would make life difficult, but manageable.

Can you accept the fact that you have some control over what happens in your life, but not 100%? Do you accept this idea intellectually and have you also processed it emotionally? This man had less control over his life than you probably do, but he was relaxed about it. He looked the tiger in the eye, turned his back, and walked away to resume what, for him, was a normal life. For some strange reason, I feel very encouraged by this man, whom I do not know, who certainly has no idea who I am, whom I have never seen, and yet, in just a few minutes on the radio, gave me a different perspective on life.

Your life purpose does not have to be complicated, in fact, it is probably not your real life purpose if it takes much more than one sentence to say what it is—why not try to write your life purpose? In the following exercise, try to write at least one important thing about the purpose of your life.

Exercise: Life Purpose

At least one of the purposes of my life is

_____

_____

_____

_____

I'll give you my version of this exercise.

At least one of the purposes of Edwin's life is to be available to help people cope with their life circumstances by understanding them and guiding them to appropriate resources. I believe amazing resources are out there for those of us who earnestly seek them.

So the last chapter of this book is not a bad place to start, when considering your dreams. However, if I had started the book with the question of your life's purpose, you may not have finished the book because this is probably the most difficult thing to do. You certainly can succeed with Dream It, Learn It, Work It without having a well thought out statement of your purpose for being alive. It is just that it eventually all comes back to purpose. In my practice as a career counselor, I see many people who have already had successful careers in one sense (they made lots of money and enjoyed high status on the job), but who were unfulfilled in another sense. They come to me because they are searching for that "other sense." They want the work they do to be congruent with who they are as a person.

Mary Jo

Mary Jo worked as an attorney in Washington D.C. She graduated from The Evergreen State College and went on to get her law degree. When she called me to seek career counseling, she said she perceived a serious mismatch between her job and her life direction. She really said something much more vague than that, but it was what I heard her say beneath her words. The general direction of her life, as it related to family and friends, was positive. But there was something missing in her work.

Mary Jo worked for a private attorney whose clients were in the entertainment industry, an industry she loved. In fact, she had made an attempt on her own time to resurrect an old theatre and stage productions in the Washington D. C. area. Ultimately, this idea did not materialize because she couldn't find sufficient financing. When she first talked to me, she was really in a quandary as to what she should do. The job was close to an industry she loved, but her boss did not give her a lead role in the business.

I suggested if she engaged in a process of self-assessment with me, we might be able to tease out details about how she could make her employment more compatible with her personal beliefs. She completed a number of exercises I suggested and with each result she came closer to understanding what she needed in a job to have a sense of fulfillment. Ultimately, I asked her to write an essay on this question: What must be present in any job for you to feel a sense of satisfaction and purposeful direction?

Mary Jo was willing to do the work honestly and we just kept inching closer and closer toward describing her ideal job and ideal job environment. She interviewed people in the entertainment industry to find out about job opportunities. She had mixed results. She let it be known among her friends in the legal community that she was looking for a change. She also began to phase herself out of her old job, both physically and emotionally. She was ready to leap.

One day, after we had completed the assessment process, she called to say she had interviewed for a job with a union that represented entertainment industry workers. She told me the employer was very interested in her background and was eager to hire her. Mary Jo had doubts. This job did not exactly fit her ideal and she was more interested in working on the producing side of entertainment, not the worker-protection side. I suggested a review of her assessment work and an analysis of how well the job description for this position met her criteria for a dream job. I thought it was a great match, but she was not so sure. She decided to take the job and give it a try, but she had misgivings because it was not precisely what she envisioned.

Several months passed before I heard from Mary Jo again. When she did email me, I was pleasantly surprised. Not only was her job going well, it wildly exceeded her expectations. She had become an important member of the union team, her opinions were sought out, her advice was followed, and she had excellent chances for promotion. The match between her ideal job and the actual job was almost perfect. Although she thanked me for my assistance, which I appreciated, I explained to her that when people are willing to do the necessary work, it makes my job easy. The information we used in her quest all came from her; I just helped her interpret the information and use it to define where she would like to go with her occupation. She did the work—I held her hand for a short stretch as she climbed her chosen trail.

Mary Jo is a good example of how your life/career direction can help you climb the mountain of your dreams. It also illustrates how you can help others up the mountain through your larger purposes in life. Mary Jo wanted to support the theatre movement in the Washington D.C. area. Her employment choice put her into a position to help people who work in the entertainment industry and put her in touch with other important people who could help her preserve and restore the theatre community.

If *who* you are is in tune with *what* you do in your life/career, then you are truly blessed.

In the career center where I work, we have a saying, one for which we have been unable to find a source, that sums up most of what I have been talking about—

BECOMING WHO YOU ARE
IS THE MOST IMPORTANT JOB YOU HAVE.

Here endeth the lesson.
Good luck to you on your journey!

. . . oh, and could you drop a postcard now and again
from the road?

E.C.B.

Appendix I:

Additional Resources for Assessment

In the field of career counseling, there are a variety of tools used for assessment. These assessment methods are designed to get to the answers of who you are and what you were put on earth to do. They tend to be quick and useful. For example, psychological type, which was developed out of the typology of psychologist Carl Jung is commonly used in assessment and yields excellent results most of the time. Various books have been written about how to convert information about type into career and life direction. One of the best is "Do What You Are" by Tieger and Barron-Tieger. With it, you can do this career assessment yourself. A short exercise near the beginning of the Tieger book will allow you to determine your personality type quickly. Follow their instructions closely, because finding your correct type is key to making this book work for you. Another way is to go to Humanmetrics.com, a web site where you can determine your "type" by taking a short test on-line. I might add, however, that using the services of a career counselor could also add depth to your understanding of the results.

Interest and skill tests are available to most career seekers through high schools, colleges and universities. Public employment agencies, federally funded Employment and Training programs (such as Washington State's WorkSource), and private career counselors will also have available a variety of assessment processes. Some of these instruments, such as "The Strong Interest Inventory" and "The Campbell Interest and Skill Survey" provide broad and useful information about jobs and occupations. Measuring your interests and your skills and then comparing them to people who work in specific occupations can give you a very good starting point. I must emphasize here that it is always up to you to validate the information for yourself. You would not want to take the results of any single assessment test as the whole truth about you and your life/career direction. These tools give you good clues about yourself and in many cases will fit you well. Remember the purpose of these assessments is to put you in the driver's seat of your life and keep you there. Always analyze what someone or something says about you and determines how much of it is true and use the parts that seem right for you. *You* are the only true authority in the world about *You.*

One of the foremost authorities on jobs and careers is Richard Bolles. His book, *"What Color is your Parachute?"* published in 1973 has been republished every year since then. Each new edition is revised and updated; it is a constant work in progress and an impressive testament to the timelessness of his message. In the parts of the book where Bolles writes about how to discover your life passions, his basic approach remains the same, regardless of which edition you read. There is an exercise in each edition of his book called "The Quick Job-Hunting Map." Although it takes a fair amount of time and effort to complete this section, the results are always useful. I would recommend reading the most current copy of *"Parachute"* you can find because Bolles' writing is uplifting and his messages clear.

"Integrative Life Planning" by L. Sunny Hansen provides an innovative look at ways in which you can combine career development with the planning for other aspects of your life. She describes, in detail, 6 Critical Tasks that you might use to investigate important areas of your life and career to gain insight about how to blend who you are with what you do. It is a well-researched, thought-provoking book that can only help you in your life journey.

Let me say in summary that each of the resources cited in this Appendix has influenced my thinking about Life/Career planning and development. It is difficult to know exactly what system or approach will work for each person seeking self-knowledge. Since we are shaped by our own education and life experience, which is never the same for any two people, each of us is a unique human being who must find our own truth. These references may be very helpful to you in that quest.

Appendix 2:

Exercise: Occupational Direction

The detailed Occupational Direction Exercise below should give you some important clues about a general focus for occupational choice, assuming that employment is one of your choices. (If paid or volunteer employment is not one of your top choices, then you may skip this exercise.) This material is adapted from O*NET and the Occupational Outlook Handbook, employment data from the U.S. Department of Labor. As you read these occupational descriptions, rate your interest in each one on a scale of 1 to 5 where 5 is most interested and 1 is least interested. Take your time. If your specific occupational interest is not listed, just make a smart guess about which category it will fall into and write it down near the correct category.

I. _____Management, business and financial operations occupations. This category of jobs includes general managers, financial managers and executives. These are managers and executives in business, government and the non-profit sectors. Whether the organization is large or small, all of these management functions must be performed, although in a smaller organization the responsibilities may be combined. If you want to be in charge, this is the place for you.

II. _____Professional and Technical occupations. Included here are financial specialists, purchasers and buyers, human resources workers, inspectors and compliance officers, management support workers, engineers, architects and surveyors, engineering technologists, physical and life scientists and technologists, computer scientists, mathematical scientists, social scientists, social service workers, religious workers, lawyers, judges and legal assistants, teachers and educators, librarians, counselors, health care workers (includes doctors, dentists, nurses, etc.), artists, writers, performers (includes athletes, trainers and coaches), and all other paraprofessional and technical workers.

III. _____Sales occupations. Sales workers include sales supervisors and managers, sales agents (real estate, travel, fund raising, floral, financial services), technical, wholesale and retail sales, sales consultants and estimators.

IV. _____Office and Administrative Support occupations. Primarily found in a business or government office setting, these occupations include administrative supervisors, financial transaction workers, insurance specialists, investigators and collectors, government clerical workers, travel and hotel clerks, library assistants, teacher aides, secretaries, and general office support workers such as receptionist, personnel/payroll clerk, typing/filing clerk, bookkeepers/accounting clerks, general office support workers, office machine operators, communication equipment operators (switchboard/information), mail clerks and carriers, scheduling and distributing workers like dispatchers, transportation agents, order fillers and engineering clerks.

V. _____Service occupations. Service supervisors and managers (police/fire supervisors, chefs and head cooks, supervision and management of service workers), private household workers, protective service workers (variety of police/fire fighter/corrections officers), food service workers, medical/dental assistants, cleaning and building service workers, personal service workers (barbers/ hair dressers/travel guides/personal and home care aides).

VI. _____Farming, fishing, and forestry occupations. This category includes agricultural farmers and workers (including organic), fishers and fishing vessel operators, and forest, conservation and logging workers.

VII. _____Installation, maintenance, and repair occupations. This broad category includes electrical/electronic equipment mechanics, installers, and repairers, vehicle and mobile equipment mechanics, installers, and repairers (automotive/diesel/small engine), line installers and repairers, heating, refrigeration, and air conditioning workers, and line installers and repairers.

VIII. _____Construction trades and related occupations. These occupations include carpenters, electricians, construction equipment operators, and drywall workers, masons, concrete workers, tile setters, and reinforcing metal workers, painters and paper hangers, plumbing workers, flooring installers, highway and rail workers, roofers, fence installers, extraction and mining, metal and plastic workers.

IX. _____Production occupations. Here we have assemblers and fabricators, food processing occupations, metal and plastics workers, aircraft systems assemblers, plant and systems operators (power plant operator, stationary engineer, treatment plant operators), printing occupations, textile, apparel and furnishings occupations, woodworkers and other productions occupations such as dental lab technicians, jewelers, vision technicians, and semi-conductor processors.

X. _____Transportation and material moving occupations. Air transportation occupations (pilots/flight engineers/air traffic controllers), material moving occupations, motor vehicle operators (bus drivers, taxi drivers, truck drivers, driver/sales workers, rail transportation occupations, and water transportation occupations.

Now that you have completed this exercise, you have yet more information about where your occupational interest lies. Here are four ways you can think about using your results.

1.) Think of yourself being self-employed in one or more of your highest rated categories

2.) Think of yourself as a small business owner operating a business in a favored occupational area

3.) Think of yourself working for an organization (private company, governmental or non-profit organization) that is small, medium or large where you are an employee, working in the occupation(s) you have chosen.

4.) Think of yourself as a volunteer for a non-profit or governmental organization.

Which one appeals to you the most? Dare to dream. In the space provided below, list your favorite occupational area(s) and how you would most like to see yourself working within that field.

Most Appealing Occupational Area(s):

1.)_____

2.)_____

3.)_____

Best Way(s) to be Employed:

1.) Self-Employed

2.) Small Business Owner

3.) Employee in a Small, Medium or Large Organization

4.) Volunteer

Made in the USA
San Bernardino, CA
29 December 2015